YORK FILM NOTES

Fear Eats the Soul

Director
Rainer Werner Fassbinder

Note by Becky Parry

Longman

Y York Press

York Press
322 Old Brompton Road, London SW5 9JH

Pearson Education Limited
Edinburgh Gate, Harlow, Essex CM20 2JE, United Kingdom
Associated companies, branches and representatives throughout
the world

Angst Essent Seele Auf © Fassbinders Filme 3, Verlag der Autoren,
Frankfurt am Main 1990
Stills © Rainer Werner Fassbinder Foundation / Fotograph: Peter Gauhe

First published 2000

ISBN 0-582-43224-3

Designed by Vicki Pacey
Phototypeset by Gem Graphics, Trenance, Mawgan Porth, Cornwall
Colour reproduction and film output by Spectrum Colour
Printed in Malaysia, KVP

contents

author of this note Becky Parry is Education Manager at the Showroom Cinema in Sheffield, the largest independent cinema outside London. Becky lives in Sheffield, where she studied Communication Studies at Sheffield Hallam University (BA Hons) and English and Media at Sheffield University (PGCE). Becky taught Media and Film Studies at Secondary and FE level and is an active member of the South Yorkshire Media Education Network.

background

trailer

The best thing I can think of would be to create a union between something as beautiful and powerful and wonderful as Hollywood films and a criticism of the status quo. That's my dream, to make such a German film.

Fassbinder, quoted in Braad Thomsen,1997, p. 24

Produced by Fassbinder's Tango Films in 1973, *Fear Eats the Soul* was shot in 18 days with a modest budget of DM 260,000. It is often cited as one of Fassbinder's most accessible films – a simple love story with universal themes. It tells the story of a marriage between an older cleaning woman, Emmi Kurowski (Brigitte Mira), and a young guest worker (*gastarbeiter*), Ali (El Hedi ben Salem). Their relationship, more solace than passionate love, is disapproved of by their wider society. The film reveals bigoted, parochial attitudes in working-class German life. These are attitudes still familiar to international audiences and thus the film retains its resonance.

The way in which *Fear Eats the Soul* anatomises German racism is only too topical now, in a climate of resurgent fascism.

Andy Medhurst, Sight and Sound, Vol. 6, No. 2, February 1996

The film represents a breakthrough for Fassbinder, winning the International Critics Prize at Cannes in 1974 and affirming his international status. The film also achieved commercial release in Europe and America, reaching the wider audiences Fassbinder sought. It was shot in between the comparatively big-budget Fassbinder productions *Martha*, made for television, and *Effi Briest.*

The film is often described as a remake of Douglas Sirk's *All That Heaven Allows* (1955) starring Jane Wyman as an older woman who falls in love with her young gardener Rock Hudson. It is useful to see the film as a tribute to all that Fassbinder loved about Hollywood films. However, he uses the film to reveal all that he dislikes about the status quo: namely xenophobic attitudes in society and the damage individuals do to each other in the name of love, alongside the constraints on Hollywood studio directors as well as those placed on New German Film makers.

> His remake of the Hollywood classic reflects the experience he had whilst watching *All That Heaven Allows.* It is not a remake of the movie itself.
>
> *Robert C. Reimer, 1996, p. 282*

Fassbinder was attempting to make explicit what he saw as hidden messages in the Douglas Sirk film. However, this is not a film of polemics: political, sexual or otherwise. Fassbinder is almost solely concerned with the notion of encouraging his audience to interpret the film actively. Thus, whilst he uses the structure of conventional melodrama to engage the audience, he relocates the story to a harsher environment, paring down the characters and settings to their simplest form. It is the stark and austere simplicity of the film that might appear to distance the audience from the lovers, but actually heightens our understanding of the coldness and hostility they face and the comfort they seek in each other.

> The coldness of *Fear Eats the Soul* is not emotionless: far from dulling the viewer it produces a profound shiver, marking the success of Fassbinder in constructing a film which will make audiences both think and feel.
>
> *Ed Lowry, in The International Directory of Films and Filmmakers, 1997, p. 51*

reading fear eats the soul

> My films are often criticised for being pessimistic. In my opinion there are enough reasons to be pessimistic, but in fact, I don't see my films like that. They developed out of the position that the revolution should take place not on the screen, but in life itself, and when I see things going wrong, I do it to make people aware that this is what happens unless they change their lives.
>
> *Fassbinder, quoted in Braad Thomsen, 1997, p. 24*

background reading fear eats the soul

Fear Eats the Soul marked a watershed for Fassbinder by gaining international commercial release as well as popular and critical acclaim. The reception of some of his earlier films had been extremely hostile, offending both left and right wing alike, and his reputation for drug use and an unconventional lifestyle dominated his own nation's awareness of him as a film maker. However, this developing reputation made him an intriguing figure to many cineasts outside Germany. Fassbinder had established a following in Europe and the USA amongst film academics and enthusiasts, but hitherto his films were screened only in festivals and occasionally at political conventions. *Fear Eats the Soul* was long awaited and received heightened critical attention.

Laura Mulvey's review of the film in the feminist publication, *Spare Rib* (no. 30, 1974), staked the claim that the genre of melodrama was relevant to Film Studies. She places Fassbinder's film and its relationship with the work of Douglas Sirk at the centre of this debate. Fassbinder discussed in depth his interpretation of Sirk and the subversive meaning he found in his use of mise-en-scène. The film has usefully contributed to the discussion of the evolution and interpretation of melodrama.

Fassbinder saw melodrama as a way of reaching his audience but in his work he regularly defies the audiences' expectations of the genre. In the opening sequence of *Fear Eats the Soul* we are introduced not to the established order of the world of the film, but to the moment at which Emmi steps out of that world and ventures into a new one. We are instantly confronted by the moment of disruption to the social order.

Emmi enters the immigrants' bar ostensibly because of the rain, but we find she has passed this way before and been intrigued by the music. The camera, positioned in the centre of the bar, cuts from one side of the room to the other looking first at Emmi, emphasising her discomfort at being in a place with which she is not familiar, and then to the regulars at the bar who sense a stranger in their midst. Fassbinder deliberately creates a tableau effect using long takes and eliciting slow and mannered movements from the actors. The room is fairly sparse, the furniture utility, yet the walls are draped with rich textiles and the music is Arabic and thus, at least in relation to Emmi, the bar is exotic. We are not given this context

The regulars at the bar
sense a stranger
in their midst

background reading fear eats the soul

by establishing scenes. The reaction of the inhabitants in the bar to the older white woman who has intruded at once sets up the social order and disrupts it.

At the time the film was made Fassbinder was in a stage of transition from his earlier work which is often cited as inaccessible and self indulgent, and his later, more sophisticated use of melodrama. This transition period was also influenced by his work in the theatre. At key moments in the film he uses the actors like frozen manikins on a stage setting. The effect is to remind us constantly of the presence of the camera and of our own role as spectators.

Fassbinder attacked both German society and the failings of humanity; his films detail the desperate yearning for love and freedom and the many ways in which society and the individual contribute to their own downfall. The story of an older woman energised by her love for a younger man is related in Fassbinder's earlier gangster film *The American Soldier*, except that in this film the story ends with a death – the murder of the older woman. This version of the story was one that Fassbinder found in a newspaper – he came across the idea for the illness that Ali suffers from through a similar account from a medical worker. It was a story that stayed with him.

Three years after its inclusion in the earlier gangster film, the story is used as the central plot for *Fear Eats the Soul*. However, those three years are important in Fassbinder's development – having spent time working in television and exploring his interest in Sirkian melodrama in an essay on the film *All That Heaven Allows*, his attitude to the possibilities of the film medium had changed:

> Before I would no doubt have told the story as it really is, with the old lady dying, because society does not let an old woman and a gastarbeiter live together. But now what I want to do is show how it is possible to defend one self and manage it, despite everything. Now I tend to think that if these depressing circumstances are only reproduced in a film, it simply strengthens them. Consequently the

> dominant conditions should be presented with such transparency
> that one understands they can be overcome.
>
> *Fassbinder, quoted in Braad Thomsen, 1997, p. 38*

Fassbinder cites the simplicity of the story as something that his television work influenced:

> We wanted to keep it so simple that people would keep thinking:
> All sorts of things would be possible. I don't consider human beings
> incapable of change. It's built into the structure of my film that
> people begin to see, Yes it is better if things are a bit different.
>
> *Fassbinder, quoted in Watson, 1996, p. 1*

key players' biographies

RAINER WERNER FASSBINDER

> I'm watching television, video and reading in between. I have some
> more things to do.
>
> *Braad Thomsen, 1997, Introduction*

Fassbinder, arguably the best-known director of the New German Cinema, is described variously as a national asset and a national disgrace, but he was undeniably a prolific film maker. Over a thirteen year period he averaged a film every 100 days and directed over 40 films between 1969 and 1982. He wrote most of his scripts, produced and edited many of his films and wrote plays and songs, as well as acting on stage, in his own films and in the films of others. He also produced a considerable body of work for television.

Fassbinder, also known as Franz Walsch, was born in 1946 in Bad Worishofen three weeks after the Americans entered the town. The division of Germany commenced. He recalled his early years as lonely and lacking in love and affection. His father, a physician, and his mother, a translator, were divorced in 1951; Fassbinder had little contact with his father after that.

> I also began to live alone very early; for example, between the ages
> of seven and nine I largely lived alone, that is, in an apartment

> where there certainly were people – because my mother who was
> ill, had sublet rooms – but there was no one there to look after me,
> there just wasn't anything except literature and art.
>
> *Fassbinder, quoted in Braad Thomsen, 1997, p. 3*

From around the age of seven, Fassbinder went to the cinema, often on his own.

> I tend to say that he slid to the movies in his nappies … To me films
> were for amusement, they were something for a Saturday
> afternoon, but not several times a day and I often thought what's
> going to become of this child who only wants amusement? But
> then I had no idea what he was teaching himself by doing it. I only
> reproached myself because I was unable to set any limits and be
> consistent about it.
>
> *Liselotte Eder (Fassbinder's mother), quoted in Braad Thomsen, 1997, p. 4*

Early on Fassbinder rejected his parental influences – the bourgeois literature and art he cites earlier is replaced in his affections by some of Hollywood's most popular directors. He is often portrayed in biographies as a rebel, perhaps because of, for example, his unashamed declaration of his homosexuality at fifteen. Clearly he sought influences outside his own domestic experience. Thomas Elsaesser, who has written extensively on both Fassbinder and New German Cinema, points out that Fassbinder may have come from a quite affluent background, but in later life situated himself with social exiles.

Fassbinder attended private and public schools at Augsburg and Munich but left before graduating in 1964 to enrol in a private drama school. In the summer of 1967 Fassbinder joined the Action Theatre, a progressive left wing theatre company, and two months later he had become the company's co-director. When it reorganised under the name 'anti-theatre', having been closed down by the state, he emerged as its leader. The group lived together and staged a number of controversial and politically radical plays in 1968 and 1969, including some of Fassbinder's original works and adaptations.

austere and minimalist in style

His attitude to the audience as an actor might reveal something about his formative years, but it also foregrounds his developing priority to engage and confront his film audience.

> I played against the audience with a direct aggressiveness, probably going to the limits of what was possible, which no doubt arose from the fear that the audience might not like me.
>
> *Fassbinder, quoted in Braad Thomsen, 1997, p. 9*

A similar attitude is reflected in his later decision to act in his own films, where he often took small character roles such as the role of Eugen in *Fear Eats the Soul*. Here, he plays the least appealing character. During his 'anti-theatre' period he made ten feature films, including *Love is Colder than Death*, *Katzelmacher*, and *Beware of the Holy Whore*. Influenced by Jean-Luc Godard, Jean-Marie Straub and the theories of Bertolt Brecht, these films are austere and minimalist in style, and although praised by many critics, they proved too demanding and inaccessible for a mass audience.

It was during this time, however, that Fassbinder developed his rapid working methods. Using actors and technicians from the 'anti-theatre' group, he was able to complete films ahead of schedule and often under budget, and in doing so compete successfully for government subsidies.

Fassbinder was driven by his commitment to attaining a mass audience with his films.

> The American cinema is the only one I can take seriously, because it's the only one that has really reached an audience.
>
> *Fassbinder, quoted in Sight and Sound, Vol. 44, No. 1, Winter 74/75, p. 2*

Fassbinder greatly admired popular Hollywood directors such as Douglas Sirk, Raoul Walsh and Michael Curtis, with whom he identified the ability to make their own creative and ideological voices heard within the constraints of the Hollywood production system.

Fassbinder's recognition as a film maker grew quickly, and in 1977 Manhattan's New Yorker Theatre held a Fassbinder festival. That same year saw the release of *Despair*. Shot in English on a budget that nearly equalled the cost of his first fifteen films, *Despair* was based on a novel by Vladimir Nabokov, adapted by Tom Stoppard, and starred Dirk Bogarde. But as enthusiasm for Fassbinder grew in Europe and the USA, his films seemed to make little impression on German audiences. At home, he was better known for his work in television, *Eight Hours are Not a Day*, the 151-hour *Berlin Alexanderplatz*, and for the notoriety surrounding his lifestyle and open homosexuality.

Coupled with the controversial issues that his films took up – terrorism, state violence, racial intolerance, sexual politics – it seemed that everything Fassbinder did provoked or offended someone. Charges levelled against him included anti-Semitism, anti-Communism, and anti-feminism. With *The Marriage of Maria Braun* (1979), Fassbinder finally attained the popular acceptance he sought, even with German audiences. The film recounts and assesses post-war German history as embodied in the rise and fall of the main character, played by Hanna Schygulla. It is a story of manipulation and betrayal which exposes Germany's spectacular post-war economic recovery in terms of its cost in human values.

In the years following *Maria Braun*, Fassbinder made 'private' films such as *In a Year of 13 Moons* and *The Third Generation*, stories that explored personal experiences, as well as big budget spectacles like *Lili Marlene* and *Lola*. By the time he made his last film, *Querelle* (1982, dedicated to Salem), heavy doses of drugs and alcohol had apparently become necessary to sustain his unrelenting work habits. When Fassbinder was found dead in a Munich apartment on 10 June, 1982, the cause of death was reported as heart failure resulting from interaction between sleeping pills and cocaine. The script for his next film, *Rosa Luxemburg*, was found next to him.

EL HEDI BEN SALEM

El Hedi ben Salem, who plays Ali, came to Germany from the mountains of North Africa, initially finding work as a bit-part actor. Salem taught himself to read, write and speak French as well as German. He met Fassbinder and became his lover. Fassbinder's relationship with Salem can be read as an attempt to atone for the victimisation which he felt Salem faced at the hands of German society. He certainly attempted to give him greater

El Hedi ben Salem

El Hedi ben Salem, who plays
Ali, came to Germany from the
mountains of North Africa, initially
finding work as a bit-part actor

status, first as a production assistant and then with the leading role in *Fear Eats the Soul*.

It was typical of Fassbinder to work with people he was entangled with in his personal life (see Contexts: Production). However, it would appear that the shooting of the film was actually a time of concentrated effort and focus for all the actors and crew, and that the atmosphere was less fractious than was usual on set. After the film was made, Salem became increasingly jealous of Fassbinder's other lovers and made several aggressive threats. One night after drinking heavily in a bar in Berlin he pulled a knife and stabbed three strangers. He was then assisted in running away by friends, and could not attend the Cannes festival screening because he was wanted by the police for attempted murder.

Fassbinder and Salem were to meet again, and indeed Fassbinder changed a scene in the film *Fox and His Friends* (1975) in order to include a scene in Morocco and offer Salem a part. At this point Salem made peace with Fassbinder, saying he had now got rid of his aggression. Several years later he hung himself in a French jail. He was only the first of Fassbinder's lovers to take his own life. Fassbinder's audiences were kept up to date with these dramatic events, but contemporary audiences are less likely to be aware of the closeness of the relationship or the consequences of their partnership. However, Fassbinder clearly draws on Salem's experiences in the way he shapes and positions the character of Ali.

BRIGITTE MIRA

Brigitte Mira was awarded the *Bundesverdienstkreuz* (the highest German decoration) in 1995 following an extensive career in both film and television. She worked with Fassbinder on *Eight Hours* for television and then *Fear Eats the Soul*, and took roles in several further Fassbinder films and television projects: *Lili Marlene* – Neighbour, *Berlin Alexanderplatz* (mini) TV series – Frau Bast, *Chinesisches Roulette* – Kast, *Satansbraten* – Walter's mother, *Angst vor der Angst* (TV) – Mother, *Mutter Küsters Fahrt zum Himmel* -Mother Küsters.

In Mira, Fassbinder was working with a well-established and well-loved actor who had a strong rapport with her audience but had passed the age at which she would usually be cast in lead female roles. Indeed Mira must have seemed an unusual casting to Fassbinder's home audience. Fassbinder clearly found working with Mira a refreshing change from some of his former collaborations, and he talks very positively about the effect she had on the realisation of the character, Emmi.

> Brigitte Mira identified very strongly with her role too, because she has a comparable relationship with a younger man. She can sense how people react.
>
> Fassbinder, quoted in Toteberg and Lensing (eds), 1992, p. 12

Brigitte Mira also won a Film Strip in Gold for Outstanding Individual Achievement at the German Film Awards (1974) for her portrayal of Emmi Kurowski.

FASSBINDER AND FILM

Fassbinder's complex personal relationships were integral to the way he made films and are reflected in the films themselves. His biography is important to gaining an understanding of his work. Many of his films were about the oppressor and the oppressed, which he saw as an extension of the problematic attitudes which children encounter from their own dominating parents. He was influenced by the work of both Freud and Marx but believed that an uprising against a repressive regime would replicate the structures that it initially opposed. His work often explored individual struggle, but always set this against a class structure which was the cause of many of the problems suffered by his characters. However, his films were not about suggesting alternative solutions and he rarely gave the audience an optimistic conclusion.

In *Fear Eats the Soul* we have an ending that goes against expectation. The final scene shows Emmi promising to look after Ali despite the doctor's conviction that he will soon be back in hospital with the same problem. This ending, if not exactly positive, shows a faith in humanity, in love and the need to look after each other which is missing in many of Fassbinder's films. Society condemns Ali to a world of stress and anxiety because of his immigrant status and yet Emmi believes that she can make a difference.

director as auteur

Braad Thomsen attributes Fassbinder's positive attitude to his recent television work, which gave him a different perspective on the potential power of the visual media. He may not have continued to have this conviction in all of his work, but what is clear is that he believed in the possibility of film to engage with an audience, forcing them to question their own experiences and perceptions. It is this belief which unifies his body of work and explains the manic pace at which he both lived and worked.

director as auteur

He was gentle and brutal, tender and cynical, self-sacrificing and egocentric: he was ruthlessly dictatorial and yet always dreamed of working in groups and collectives. He was obese, unkempt, slovenly, went round in a leather jacket and looked like a boozer in the bar on the corner.

Braad Thomsen, 1997, p. 1

Auteur theory, as proposed by Andrew Sarris, attempts to subjugate European film. Sarris, writing in 1968 at a time when *Cahiers du Cinema* had become disillusioned with the theory and turned to political, ideological and structuralist approaches to film analysis, proposes that American cinema is in fact the only cinema worth discussing. Sarris described a range of criteria by which a film maker could be judged an auteur: a recognisable personal vision which consistently reflected a particular worldview, directorial competence, a distinct visual style and an interior meaning, which arose from the tension between the director and the mode of production. It can certainly be strongly argued that despite working within the structures of a range of genres, Fassbinder's work offered a consistent vision of the world in which personal struggle is set against a class-bound society.

The vast body of work he produced can be read as 'authored' by him if we look solely in terms of the instrumental role Fassbinder took in the production process. *Fear Eats the Soul*, which he not only directed, acted in and was also the production designer for, was funded by Tango Films, his

low budgets and swift pace of film making

own company. It was typical of the way Fassbinder made films that he would write, edit and also produce. Added to this he created his own distinctive production system which placed on him, as director, its own constraints. He set tight deadlines, worked to small budgets and with a certain group of actors and crew with whom there were often personal entanglements to be grappled with (see Contexts: Production). Fassbinder was able 'to take control of the process of production and express his own personal concerns' (Pam Cook, 1985, p. 114).

Themes he regularly returned to include surveillance, sadomasochism and racial hatred. He also gained a reputation for pushing back many boundaries concerning the representation of homosexuality. The titles of two of his films reveal these thematic links: *Love is Colder than Death* (1969) and *I Only Want You to Love Me* (1976). His main characters, either male or female, are faced with a series of confrontations that rob them of any romantic illusions and often reveal their own ability to be cruel and manipulative.

There can also be no arguments about Fassbinder's ability to fill a scene with meaning and fascinate his audience with their interpretation of it. The skilled use of mise-en-scène arose more from his formative years in the theatre, where props and costumes and positioning were carefully constructed to express new ideas, than the constraints to which Sarris refers which influenced the work of Hollywood directors. Fassbinder, however, also had to face his own distinctive set of constraints, some imposed by the state funding system but some of his own creation. Thomas Elsaesser makes an important point about the distinction between the concept of the film maker as an avant-garde auteur with a desire to innovate, and the economic conditions within which he / she may work. The low budgets and swift pace of film making are distinguishable in many of Fassbinder's early films. Whilst we might recognise a distinctive style, we must also understand how that style developed due to pragmatic and economic constraints, and look at it alongside the work of other film makers working in similar conditions.

That these constraints caused heightened tension and impacted both on the style and form of Fassbinder's work is clear. Despite the fact that

manipulate our genre expectations

Sarris lays out these criteria to promote the superiority of US cinema, they can be applied to Fassbinder. The question remains of what this approach contributes to our understanding of film. This can be expounded if we look at the concept of directorial competence. Fassbinder's use of camera and editing when compared to his own Hollywood favourite Sirk could be described as stilted, mechanised and cold. To some this is a deliberate attempt to contrast with the seamless camerawork of his Hollywood equivalent, to others it might appear technically disappointing.

The interpretation is subjective. It is also culturally specific; that is to say, to an audience whose only film experience is mainstream Hollywood, it is easy to condemn and dismiss a film maker such as Fassbinder because of the difficulty in engaging with the ways in which he seeks to manipulate our genre expectations. Fassbinder would no doubt disappoint Hollywood audiences for whom the pleasure of film watching is to have expectations confirmed and rewarded predictably.

Pam Cook raises a valuable question in her appraisal of Sarris: is evaluation based on whether a body of work is consistent in the way it presents the world the most productive way to judge a film? This reveals the reliance of auteur theory on the model of production of the Hollywood studio system, whereby the films of a director are scrutinised to find a common world view: a subversive view which is masked by the need to meet the demands of a capitalist studio system. Auteur theory, whilst limited in use in the study of film makers outside this system, does raise some interesting parallels between Fassbinder and his own Hollywood hero, Sirk (see Contexts: Filmography).

During his lifetime, and since, the fascination with Fassbinder's lifestyle has been equal at least to that of his work. This had an impact on his audience following, and his work was quickly identified with him as the sole author rather than a product of the industry within which he worked. Fassbinder can be viewed to a degree as a star director (see Contexts: Fassbinder's audience) whose name elicited a series of expectations from his audience regarding the content and style of his films.

Elsaesser, discussing New German Cinema, points out that the director's need to self-promote is interlinked not just with the concept of auteur but

inadequacy of the camera in revealing truth

also that of film movements. Fassbinder desired wide audiences, and identified with those very US directors whose work was held in high esteem as having achieved auteur status despite the constraints of the studio system:

> That's what I saw for the first time in Sirk: apparently under the conditions of a completely different system which all revolves around money, you can still come up with something very individual and personal.
>
> *Fassbinder, quoted in Toteberg and Lensing (eds), 1992, p. 42*

It could be argued that Fassbinder set about to produce a 'romantic' image of himself as the tortured artist, and manipulated the events of his life to assist him in reaching wider audiences. He certainly did little to discourage the personalised nature of attacks on his work. He seemed to invite it, in fact, by his aggressively anti-bourgeois lifestyle, and in the various ways he acted out in public the role of super-genius who could be as ugly and spiteful as he wanted.

In summary, Fassbinder's visual style ensures that we are aware of the presence of the camera, that these are actors and that the sets are artifice. This aim, which translates to a distinctive, apparently exaggerated and mechanistic style (see Style), reflects an attempt to communicate with an audience whose cinematic experience is dominated by Hollywood. By using the syntax of a popular Hollywood genre, melodrama, Fassbinder sets up certain expectations in his audience. When these expectations are not realised, the audience becomes engaged in questioning the motives of the characters, but Fassbinder refuses to offer simplistic solutions and, coupled with his audience's awareness of artifice, the inadequacy of the camera in revealing truth is highlighted. The only truth available to the audience is a reflection of their own experience. This can be frustrating to a new viewer of Fassbinder who is used to being offered a series of solutions (see Narrative & Form: Narrative). However, it is this relationship with the audience which makes it useful to study his body of work and seek out his authorial signatures.

narrative & form

narrative

In the classic narrative, events in the story are organised around a basic structure of enigma and resolution. At the beginning of the story, an event may take place which disrupts a pre-existing equilibrium in the fictional world. It is then the task of the narrative to set up a new equilibrium.

Annette Kuhn, in Pam Cook (ed), 1985, p. 212

Fassbinder's interest in both Hollywood and melodrama is reflected in his use of classic realist narrative conventions. The term classic, in this sense, refers to repetitive use of recognisable structures. It is not a value judgement about the cultural worth of a particular set of films. The word realist, in this context, does not refer to documentary or social realist film making but the way in which Hollywood film makers developed structures and forms which present the audience with a visual world which is both believable and consistent. Narrative structure is extremely important to the establishment of verisimilitude, that is to say, a world that appears to conform to the expectations of the audience.

Debate about film narrative is influenced by the work of Vladimir Propp and focuses on recognition and analysis of discernible structures or patterns. Propp published, in 1928, an analysis of a large number of Russian folk and fairy stories and found what he described as universal patterns. This work was later applied by film theorists to Hollywood film, and, in particular, generic film. Patterns of storylines can be found which link characters with a chain of events and lead to a predictable conclusion. Narrative is therefore predictable and is the mechanism used by film makers to build the audience's expectations. Film makers therefore have at their disposal the audience's experiences of storytelling in film, literature and other forms which assist them in recognising and predicting events.

In film these conventions include events which are linked logically and causally and follow on, one from the other, in a linear fashion. Closure in classic Hollywood narrative is extremely important – ends are tied up. There is a high degree of inevitability to the resolution. Therefore in melodrama the ending might involve the marriage of the central lovers or their final parting. These endings are unambiguous and offer pleasures linked to the re-establishment of a recognisable order. In the use of both camera and editing a fictional world is created which we, as the audience, are able to understand. It is believable although not necessarily realist in the same way that a documentary would be.

Editing is hugely important and demonstrates the difference between the believable and the real. Shots are linked together to take us from place to place with almost seamless movement. These filmic devices evolved over time and became established codes; for example, the eye-line match in editing establishes the relationship between the characters and ensures spatial and temporal consistency. The camera obeys the 180 degree line rule, again ensuring the audience are not confused by where they are positioned in relation to the action.

In the case of Fassbinder it is worth considering the way in which he observed many narrative rules whilst subverting others. Producing films at a time when new ideas were being explored in film theory and practice, Fassbinder was influenced by the work of Godard – a film maker who set out to subvert many of the established rules of Hollywood cinema. Fassbinder was part of the New German Cinema along with contemporaries such as Straub and Huillet who attempted to produce a 'counter-cinema', that is to say, a cinema that confronted the audience with a less comfortable experience. They did not observe narrative rules and events did not always follow the expected linear pattern.

The films often presented problematic, ambiguous or simply unresolved endings, leaving audiences potentially estranged from the characters. The central aim of these films was different from conventional Hollywood films – they were political and not about producing pleasure. They were confrontational and deliberately difficult. It is perhaps the lack of commercial success or Fassbinder's greater concern with telling stories that led him to the compromise that is *Fear Eats the Soul.*

The film follows established traditions of Hollywood narrative so that events follow a logical sequence, but often the amount of film time given to key moments is unconventional. The equilibrium of Emmi's world is disrupted by her love for Ali. The relationship is at first threatened from the outside by the hostile racist reactions of work colleagues, family and neighbours. Once this disruption is resolved the lovers face internal conflict which is, at least to some extent, resolved once Emmi learns that she must love without making excessive demands. However, the end of the film reintroduces the role of society and although there is a high degree of closure – the lovers are reunited – the film also leaves us with the sense that the internal world of the lovers will always be subject to further disruption.

Fassbinder thus distinguishes himself from other New German Cinema directors. However, he does so in a way that flouts the expectations we might have of melodrama. This is particularly true of Fassbinder's portrayal of Emmi, who is a decisive protagonist whose actions mark her out as very different from the Jane Wyman character in *All That Heaven Allows.*

Emmi is the principal causal agent in the film and is endowed with consistent traits, qualities, and behaviour. These are established early in the film. She is a mother and a widow who cares for her family, she is a good cook, she makes strong coffee and she appears kind. She is also apparently lonely and thus tempted to be more adventurous than we might expect of a woman of her age and class. She acts quickly and decisively and she does not deliberate over decisions. Her goals are initially clear – she seeks love – and within the first third of the film she has already married and introduced her new husband to her family. It could be argued that Fassbinder rather takes the wind out of the sails of the narrative because he resolves so much so quickly. This contrasts with our expectations of melodrama where the central character usually stalls the action of the film with his or her deliberations.

Melodrama of the 1950s, as typified by films such as Sirk's *Written on the Wind* and *Tarnished Angels*, positions the (then largely female) audience to identify with the central character, a woman. This identification with the protagonist leads us to hope that the decisions she eventually makes will result in her happiness. This is not always the case, as in *Brief Encounter* where the mother returns to the family: this decision is right by society but it does not obey the rules of romantic love. Initially, in *All That Heaven Allows*, Jane Wyman makes a similar decision to reject her lover, but an accident reunites them allowing us to have added sympathy because he is 'damaged' and needs her. The conventions of melodrama dictate that the narrative is intricately linked with the decision-making of the central character, who usually suffers great angst in attempting to combine her own wishes with those of her family.

In *Fear Eats the Soul* we do not have time to ponder over Emmi's decision to either sleep with Ali or marry him. Emmi's character drives the action. They have sex, move in together and get married in the space of weeks, possibly days. This is in stark contrast to the traditions of melodrama, and shifts the tension away from the conventional climax centred on the future status of the relationship. Fassbinder strips away this function by presenting each decision as if it were entirely natural; the inevitable consequences of mutual love.

Prior to the marriage, the reactions of Emmi's society are indicated in a series of scenes where Emmi tests the water. Krista, Emmi's daughter, and her son-in-law, Eugen, laugh and scoff at the very thought of their mother in love and dismiss the idea as if she is mad. Emmi gauges their reaction to immigrant workers and is not surprised at the racist attitude revealed by Eugen (played by Fassbinder himself). Her work colleagues bitterly discuss the threatening sexuality and dirtiness of Arabs, and her neighbours observe her actions with a scandalised demeanour. The consequences are clearly implied, but Emmi is not deterred. We, the audience, are surprised at the speed of their union, but then the force of the hostility which the pair face on announcing their marriage equally surprises us, ensuring our empathy for them.

There is a sense in which Fassbinder is playing with the way we link marriage or union with resolution in film. Here the marriage is only the start of the difficulties faced by the characters. This allows us to see another side to both Emmi and Ali after they are married and the initial reactions to their relationship have died down. Once the external forces, which put pressure on the relationship, are broken down, the protagonists turn upon each other. Emmi, as the dominant figure, shows herself capable of both cruelty and the same kind of cultural small-mindedness as her fellow workmates. For example, she refuses to cook couscous and tells Ali he should eat German food now. She shows off his physical strength and cleanliness, playing to the preconceptions of her neighbours.

> Emmi opens out, gradually loses her own fears and draws close to Ali while confronted by the outright hostility of the others, but then she becomes more remote from him as she is absorbed by the affable prejudice.
>
> *Richard Combs, Monthly Film Bulletin, Nov 1974, p. 244*

We now see both characters acting archetypal roles. Initially, Emmi is the oppressor but as a consequence of Ali's drinking and taking of a lover, she is re-presented as a victim – the abandoned wife crying on the staircase. The fact that Ali turns to the bar owner Barbara, who offers to make him couscous and is clearly sexually available to him, shows a lack of passion. She offers him comfort – he is lonely and craves warmth and acceptance. This is particularly evident in the scene where he is shown in silhouette, almost mechanically removing his clothes and standing awkwardly before they have sex. Ali is capable of great cruelty too: when Emmi seeks him out at work and his workmates laugh and mock her, he joins in the laughter, deliberately setting out to hurt her.

True to classic realist closure it is important that the main character can learn and change, often through conflict. We see Emmi come to an understanding that the love she has for Ali must include kindness. She arrives at this decision before he collapses in her arms. She also believes that together they can be strong and recognises the great anxiety in him. Ali tells Emmi that the phrase 'fear eats the soul' is one that Arabs often use; certainly fear is eating his soul. The film's ending is sudden and unexpected; a reflection of the unendurable tension Ali experiences as a

Ali turns to the bar owner Barbara

Ali turns to the bar owner
Barbara, who offers to make
him couscous and is clearly
sexually available to him

stranger in a hostile land. However, Emmi is able to suggest a solution: 'When we're together, we must be nice to one another.'

It is clear that Fassbinder is a film maker who utilises the narrative conventions of Hollywood classic realist films. However, he subverts these conventions enough to ensure that his films confront his audience with a harsher reality than they might normally expect. This is almost certainly a result of the combination of influences on his work but it also emphasises his understanding of and relationship with the audience.

character

EMMI

> All in all, I find that women behave just as despicably as men do, and I try to illustrate the reasons for this: namely, that we have been led astray by our upbringing and by the society we live in.
>
> Fassbinder, quoted in Braad Thomsen, 1997, p. 30

The character Emmi is markedly different from many of Fassbinder's portrayals of women. For example, in *The Bitter Tears of Petra von Kant*, adapted from his play of the same name, Petra (Margit Carstensen), a 'classy' autocrat whose marriage has failed, falls for Karin (Hanna Schygulla), a beautiful working-class model. Karin's exploitation of Petra mirrors Petra's extraordinary psychological abuse of her silent maid, Marlene (Irm Hermann). Although Emmi shares Petra's desperate need for love, she is not capable of the level of cruelty displayed so often by both men and women, gay and straight, in Fassbinder's films. His philosophy was, on the whole, bleak. Film critic Thomas Elsaesser called it 'a cinema of vicious circles' (in Pam Cook (ed.), 1985, p. 75). Thus, a typical situation in a Fassbinder film involved a dominating figure (parent, spouse, boss) who makes sadistic demands on, betrays, deceives or abandons the protagonist, who, for some reason, is unable to escape the domination. But the antagonist also has little control over his or her actions, possessing complex, sometimes unconscious, motives. 'What the films ultimately appeal to,' Elsaesser says, 'is a solidarity between victims'. This reflects some of the pleasures elicited by melodrama. In *Fear Eats the Soul* we do see

character

inner strength and conviction

some evidence of a see-saw of cruelty similar to that described above, but Emmi in particular is much more sympathetic because Fassbinder instils her with the ability not to conform:

> in *Fear Eats the Soul* Fassbinder draws one of his rare portraits of a woman who is capable of breaking out of the traditional pattern, thereby making contact with herself.
>
> *Braad Thomsen, 1997, p. 137*

It is Emmi who visits the bar and Emmi who invites Ali up to her apartment.

```
Come on. We're all forever saying 'but'. 'But' and
everything stays the same. Stuff and nonsense. You
come upstairs with me right now. I've even got a
bottle of cognac.
```

In melodrama character traits are often assigned along traditional gender lines, giving male and female characters those traditional qualities deemed 'appropriate' to their roles in romance. However, both Sirk and Fassbinder portray women with inner strength and conviction. Jane Wyman, a star who acted in several of Sirk's melodramas, developed a persona of exterior calm crispness which contrasted with her inner turmoil. Emmi is presented more simply as no better or worse than those around her. However, her decision-making, although it emphasises Ali's comparatively low status in German society, also implies a woman able to act completely on the basis of her strength of feeling. It is interesting that both Wyman and Mira are cast in romantic leads late in their careers, neither fitting into established conventions of female beauty. Both were acclaimed for their performances in their respective films and continued to work successfully in later life in film and television. Both developed a persona linked with their roles in melodrama which female audiences especially identified with.

ALI

By positioning Ali as Fassbinder does in the opening bar scene, the hierarchy of the characters is quickly established. He is a lead character – the contrast here to the opening scenes of *All That Heaven Allows* is interesting, because Fassbinder read considerable significance into the fact

28FEAR EATS THE SOUL

victim of society's oppression

that Rock Hudson, playing Ron Kirby, was sidelined in the opening of the film. 'In the background stands Rock Hudson, blurred in the way an extra usually stands around in a Hollywood film ... Rock has no real significance yet' (Fassbinder, quoted in Reimer, 1996). Hudson is given little status, reflecting the character's role as a servant to the household.

> Ali is handled throughout by the German characters, and so never emerges as a real individual party to the confrontation.
>
> *Richard Combs, Monthly Film Bulletin, Nov 1974, p. 244*

In *Fear Eats the Soul*, the prominence given to Ali reflects his position in the hierarchy of the film narrative, not his character's social position, which is the lowest of the low. Fassbinder is encouraging the audience to identify with Ali without first presenting him as a victim of society's oppression. He establishes Ali first in his own domain, a bar frequented by his friends, and it is Emmi who is incongruous. Ali appears dignified, well liked and calm. When Ali asks Emmi to dance, he does so with no reservation or mocking humour, despite being egged on to do so by a girl at the bar whose sexual advances he has just refused.

Ali's attractive appearance is highlighted in the first sequence of the film. However, Fassbinder refrains from conventional ways of gaining the audience's sympathy for Ali. He uses few close-ups and does not give us any situation where we see Ali acting courageously or passionately, but he does gain our identification with his central character by the very lack of ostentation. Ali dresses in a sombre suit prompting Emmi to suggest he wear lighter colours which are more cheerful. The point is that he is smartly dressed and wears the conventional clothes that we later see worn by the sons of Emmi and the respectable German landlord. Ali is only seen in work clothes later, when Emmi goes to visit him at the garage.

We also see him shower and dress, but these scenes, shot as they are in long shot through frames of doorways, are not voyeuristic. We are not encouraged to linger over Ali's body – even when Emmi says, 'You are very handsome, Ali', she says it with a quietness and sorrow that implies it is regretful and that this might lead to complications, contrasting as it does with her own rounded and aged body. We should not miss Fassbinder's

lack of sexual drive

inclusion of this and several images and references to Ali washing. Robert C. Reimer (1996, p. 283) reads this as 'an ironic answer to the epithet dirty foreigner'. He also argues that Fassbinder 'exploits the homoeroticism of his star's body', linking this with the idea that Fassbinder is putting Ali, the threatening male foreign presence, 'in the face' of his audience.

It is important to note the lack of sexual drive displayed by Ali, not only to Emmi, but to Barbara and a girl in the bar. When we see Ali stroking Emmi's hand, it is not a scene of seduction. It could be argued that Fassbinder renders him impotent, but it is obviously most important that we see him as someone seeking comfort. What does Fassbinder want the audience to feel about Ali? We are not asked to admire him or gaze upon him or pity him. He is presented unequivocally as a lead character with whom we should identify. He shows humour and integrity. He displays a very unthreatening image of masculinity which it would be hard to believe could offend anyone.

There is nothing in the way Ali is presented to us that implies he is concerned with anything other than working to live. His actions are pared down to a minimum. He asks Emmi to accept money to cover his expenses. He talks with affection about his homeland and family. He talks with detachment of his situation with work – the bitterness we hear is not tinged with any sense that political or social change are imperative. He accepts. Just as he accepts Emmi's accidental marriage proposal. Just as he accepts couscous and love-making. It is what happens to him. He is passive.

The way Fassbinder positions his leading man is to give us little we cannot identify with. Ali is all of us in the way that we live our lives, perhaps thinking society should change and improve, but that day-to-day there is little we can do.

Fassbinder is situating his audience to sympathise with Ali rather than the character he plays himself, who is entirely unreasonable and bigoted. He appears to have a concept of his audience that includes the possibility that the very people who might hold the same views as Eugene might also be watching the film, and be forced to confront their own convictions. He claimed to want to 'learn how to show the audience the things they don't want to see in such a way that they will watch'.

'German master, Arab dog.'

It seems to me that the simpler a story is, the truer it is. The common denominator for many stories is as simple as this. If we'd made the character of Ali more complicated, the audience would have had a harder time dealing with the story. If the character had been more complex, the child-like quality of the relationship between Ali and Emmi would have suffered.

Fassbinder, quoted in Toteberg and Lensing (eds), 1992, p. 11

It is crucial to an understanding of the film that Fassbinder's intentions in relocating the story are understood. He not only demonstrates how universal the theme of love is, he also attempts to address the impact Ali and Emmi's social world has on them and the possibilities for their relationship. Race and age separate the two characters, but they have both class and lack of status in common. When Emmi shyly confesses she is a building cleaner, she says many people look down on her for that. Ali, whose German is limited, expresses his position more directly: 'German master, Arab dog.'

EUGEN

On first watching *Fear Eats the Soul* we notice the son-in-law, rather menacingly played by Fassbinder, whose arrogance, racism and sexism render him entirely the most unpleasant character in the film. It could be argued in favour of the film's continued pertinence that this character could just as easily appear in a contemporary British soap opera as a tabloid reading, anti-European, unhappily married, reluctantly working bloke. It is also true to say that this character above all the others stands in counterpoint to the lovers. He has no love or respect for his wife, as demonstrated by his sharp orders.

EUGEN:

> Bring me a beer.

Although we see him only briefly, we understand the world he inhabits is both suspicious and selfish:

EUGEN:

> What I do in my own house is my own business.

'He just can't accept it.'

The interchange resulting from Emmi's question about foreign workers reveals Fassbinder's understanding of the nature of racism:

KRISTA:

> Don't start on guest workers, for God's sake. Makes him see red.

EMMI:

> Why?

EUGEN:

> Because they are all pigs.

EMMI:

> I see.

EUGEN (*Shouting*):

> Yes!

KRISTA:

> His foreman at the factory is a Turk, you see. He just can't accept it.

EUGEN:

> It's nothing to do with accepting it! I don't even know he's there. He doesn't even exist!

KRISTA:

> And when he tells you to do something?

EUGEN:

> He never tells me to do nothing.

KRISTA:

> He does tell you to do things.

EUGEN:

> I just ... Get me my fags!

Eugen (Fassbinder) orders
his own wife to do things
to make himself feel better

Fassbinder offers up this representation of a working-class man who is threatened by the ability of a foreign worker and who orders his own wife to do things to make himself feel better. He thus implies the reasons for these attitudes are linked with Eugen's own lack of status, respect and power in society. By making him so repellent he does not, even by offering this explanation, give the audience any inclination towards sympathy. He exists in opposition to the lovers but his opposition is not of value to them.

OTHER CHARACTERS

Not all of the peripheral characters are so unsympathetic. Gruber the landlord's son is quite reasonable, and does not permit the reactions of the neighbours to be inflamed into any action. The police who are called out by the neighbours to protest about the loud music from Emmi's flat appear quite sympathetic. One has long hair and they ask Emmi to turn down the music respectfully. Likewise, the doctor who tells Jane Wyman in *All That Heaven Allows* that there is no medicine for her complaint has his counterpart in the final scene of *Fear Eats the Soul*.

Fassbinder changed his original draft ending for the film in which Emmi was to be killed and Ali sought by the police to include a bedside scene similar to the one in *All That Heaven Allows*. Making explicit the social illness that has laid the hero low, the doctor tells Emmi: 'Foreign workers suffer from a specific stress. It's pretty hopeless.'

The majority of the characters not within the close family who are outraged by Emmi and Ali's relationship are women. Women who stand in corridors or sit on stairwells and gossip; women who wait for their neighbours to pass to ask them favours, who watch what is happening on the street through windows, who stand around passing judgement. These woman are more typical of the way that Fassbinder usually presented female characters than Emmi is. They are cruel and bigoted.

EMMI:

> One of them tried to talk to me today, just
> imagine, me, an old woman. In the Underground.
> A gastarbeiter wanted to buy me a coffee.

'Rogues the lot of them.'

PAULA:

> There's nothing they won't try.

FRIEDA:

> Dirty pigs the lot of them. The way they live.
> Whole families live in a single room. All
> they're after is money.

EMMI:

> Perhaps they can't get a decent flat.

PAULA:

> Come on. They're tight-fisted, that's all.
> Tight-fisted pigs who don't wash. Apart from
> that, all they've got in their heads is women,
> from morning to night.

EMMI:

> But they work. That's why they are here
> because they're working.

HEDWIG:

> That's nonsense, Emmi. Just go to the station
> and take a good look. Rogues the lot of them.
> Not one of them works.

PAULA:

> Exactly. They live here because we pay them.
> And just take a look at the paper. Every day
> there's stuff about rapes and things.

EMMI:

> But there are even German women who are
> married to gastarbeiters. There are, aren't
> there?

FRIEDA:

> Sure. There are always some women who will
> stop at nothing.

'Dirty whores!'

PAULA:

> I would be ashamed. I really would be ashamed.
> Well, just the thought of it.

FRIEDA:

> But I've always said they're whores, to get
> mixed up with something like that. Dirty
> whores!

HEDWIG:

> There's one lives near us – 50 at least.
> She goes out with a Turk or something. He's
> much younger than she is. But nobody talks
> to her any more, not a soul. That's what
> she gets.

EMMI:

> Perhaps he talks to her and she doesn't need
> others at all.

PAULA:

> Nobody can do that – live without other
> people. Nobody, Emmi.

FRIEDA:

> Anyway, what can you talk about to one of
> them? They don't understand German, most of
> them. Not a word.

PAULA:

> Exactly. And anyway they just want to get
> women into bed.

HEDWIG:

> But some women like it that way. They're
> just not civilised. They've got sex on
> their brain. I would be ashamed if I was
> like that.

theme

LOVE AND DAMAGE

Once relieved of social pressure which brought the lonely Ali and Emmi together, they find their personal relationship determined by many of the same types of prejudices and assumptions, playing out their types and becoming more like those who despised them.

Ed Lowry, in The International Directory of Films and Filmmakers, 1997, p. 51

As discussed earlier (see Narrative & Form: Narrative) the theme of the oppressor and the oppressed is a recurrent in Fassbinder's work, and yet in this film the conclusion focuses our attention on society. The individual, Emmi, believes that them being kind to each other will help to alleviate Ali's suffering. The doctor believes the situation is hopeless based on his experience of the many cases he has seen before.

What emerges is a scathing critique of social repression seen from the lowest rung of society's ladder.

ibid.

RACISM

The way in which *Fear Eats the Soul* anatomises German racism is only too topical now.

Andy Medhurst, Feb 1996, p. 20

Fassbinder uses the film to explore openly racist attitudes which seem particularly shocking in Germany after the Second World War. We see something of the world Emmi lives in, and hear the casual racist conversations of her fellow cleaners, who talk about how filthy the foreign workers are. In later films Fassbinder goes on to explore further the post-Nazi attitudes of Germany. Here, we see the sort of racial prejudice which is tolerated by society because it is on the whole inactive. Yet his harsh and inhuman portrayal of the characters who display racist attitudes prompts the audience to condemn them, not to understand.

COMPROMISE

Emmi Kurowski's first husband was a Polish worker in Germany. When they see her with a Moroccan, the neighbours mutter, 'She's not a real German with that name'. However, once they return from their holiday Emmi is quickly approached for a favour which involves Ali lending a hand to shift some furniture. The grocer and his daughter snub Ali, but soon realise they need the business, and flatter Emmi to get her back in the store. Bruno, the son, sends a cheque for the smashed TV set and turns up to ask his mother to babysit every afternoon. These effects are examples of Fassbinder at his bleakest in relation to human nature. The acceptance the lovers receive is given not because of fundamental changes in attitude, but because 'society' needs a favour.

style

mise-en-scène

Fassbinder's mise-en-scène in *Fear Eats the Soul* is influenced by his desire
to locate the story in a world that is recognisable as 'real'. Thus, it is perhaps
the mise-en-scène that most markedly differentiates traditional
melodrama from Fassbinder's use of the genre. He borrows from the
iconography but does not replicate the overall mise-en-scène. Although
the home is the predominant setting of the film, it is the home of a poor
cleaner, not that of a middle-class family.

In Sirk's many melodramas for Universal, home is a lavish and gorgeous
setting which reveals a great deal about the protagonist and her life.
Colour is luxuriant and order is established by the efficient function of the
domestic setting. Nonetheless through imaginative use of mise-en-scène
we see simmering repression beneath the surface.

By adopting the classic realist mode of traditional Hollywood melodrama
Fassbinder accedes to the desire to present realism at some moments, but
then at others to remind the audience that what they are seeing is artifice.
This contradiction is rooted in what Fassbinder himself says about the
influence of Hollywood on his work:

> The main thing to be learned from American films was the need to
> meet their entertainment factor half way.
>
> *Fassbinder, quoted in Sight and Sound, Vol. 44, No. 1, Winter 74/75, p. 2*

In *Fear Eats the Soul* the settings, props and costumes locate the story in
the world of the immigrant and the cleaning woman. The bar, the opening
setting of the film, contains dark, exotic paintings and is lit and coloured
in soft, warm colours. It remains a sparse backdrop to the lovers' first

meeting. Fassbinder emphasises the fact that this is Ali's territory by using rich reds in the textiles and drapes on show.

However, underlying these superficial artefacts is the fact that this is a German bar where one can have coke or beer the same as anywhere else. Its exoticness is superficial. The tables and chairs have a utilitarian feel to them, as does the lack of personalising features elsewhere in the room. This sparseness and visual austerity are the defining elements in Fassbinder's overall approach to mise-en-scène in the film and are discussed in further detail here, under subheadings.

set design and setting

Fear Eats the Soul largely centres on Emmi's own home and related domestic settings. Each of the interior settings has the feel of a stage set. Emmi's apartment is bright white and, although it lacks the warm colour of the bar, it is not cold and stark in the same way as the stairwells and street appear. Her home is small and compact and certainly not luxurious, but it has a sense that everything has a place.

Emmi's kitchen features a childish farmyard view, which emphasises a certain naïveté in her character. It has a neatness and unused feel which perhaps reflect the ordered existence of one living alone, but also imply a stage set where none of life's debris have been allowed to accumulate. This is paralleled in Barbara's flat where Ali goes for couscous and sex. The room is white but has more modern decoration, with exotic pictures and red curtains that tie it in with the bar which Barbara owns.

The entirely clean and ordered feel is replicated in the apartment of Emmi's daughter, Krista. Although this apartment is bright and ordered, it does not attempt to reveal a great deal about the characters that inhabit it. The characters are more important than the detail of setting, which is kept in the background just as it would be in the theatre. It also fair to say that Fassbinder's choice of locations and set design were influenced by the low budget and short deadline to which he was working. These are not sets which have been long deliberated over – they are functional to the story, and it is in the exterior shots that we see Fassbinder use his creative energy (see Framing).

When Ali and Emmi dance,
the lighting changes to soft red
to give them more privacy
and signify romance

lighting

The film is lit in a naturalistic mode emphasising the everydayness of the setting. When it is night time the lighting takes on the harshness of artificial lighting, particularly in the corridor where Emmi first asks Ali to come upstairs to shelter from the rain. Here the stark grey-white of the walls contrasts with the shadows cast by the stair banisters and the doorway. Ali remains at a distance from Emmi and goes in and out of focus in accordance with Emmi's gaze. Whilst focus is used here in a very noticeable attempt to signify the distance between the two characters, lighting functions as an element of stability – it is as we expect it to be in accordance with audience experiences of classic film realism.

Occasionally changes in the lighting of the film are very obviously part of the action but also function to convey meaning. Thus, when Ali and Emmi first dance, Barbara alters the lighting on the dance floor to a softer red, which gives them more privacy from the stares of others and is clearly a colour associated with romance.

acting style

Fear Eats the Soul was made at a time when Fassbinder was still relatively new to television and actively involved in theatre, thus the film reflects an experimental stage in his use of melodrama:

> I thought that the things I was achieving with actors in the theatre could be tried out in film: you find out what you can take from one medium to benefit the other.
>
> *Fassbinder, quoted in Sight and Sound, Vol. 44, No. 1, Winter 74/75, p. 2*

Fassbinder wanted to replicate the way actors were used in the theatre and this leads to the mannered and mechanistic performances of all the characters at key moments in the film. This is most marked in the first scene, where the actors stand frozen to the spot for long periods in a kind of tableau which marks out the difference between Emmi and the others in the bar.

The actors are shot from the centre of the room in a shot reverse shot structure, though Fassbinder does not attempt to use close up to establish point of view, and the actors resemble manikins in the confined space of a stage set. When Emmi comes into the bar toward the end and requests 'that gypsy song' she and Ali first danced to, the song acts as Ali's cue, and he stands, walks toward her and asks her to dance, as if he were a robot triggered by the song.

metonym

The dominant metonym of the film is the television set, although we never see the television being watched and it is not placed in a prominent position within the room. However, a link is made with the film *All That Heaven Allows* in which a television is presented to Jane Wyman as a Christmas present but also as a replacement for the lover she has abandoned. Her son clearly believes she should be delighted with the present – our ironic knowledge of the character gives a greater ability to empathise. The television symbolises the fact that society clearly feels that mothers past a certain age should not express sexual desire, or indeed have any kind of life of their own which is not entirely dictated by the norms of society.

In *Fear Eats the Soul* the television comes to symbolise the impotence of the family, including the oldest son who kicks the screen in. There is no obvious reason for the television to be his object of anger – but it demonstrates a certain impotence. It is too late: Emmi has already married her lover, thus he kicks in the screen. In Sirk's film the television is given patronisingly to fill the need of a mother for love. In Fassbinder's film, the television is an established domestic object and the brutal action of the son reflects Emmi's harsher reality.

> My story is set in a coarse more brutal world: the same story in Sirk's film unfolds in smalltown America, where it works better. Yet the process of giving a television set instead of a man appears much more brutal against the brutal act in my film.
>
> *Fassbinder, quoted in Toteberg and Lensing (eds), 1992, p. 42*

However, Fassbinder also uses this moment to stall the audience from engaging with the narrative or the emotional states of the two central characters. Instead he draws our attention to ourselves gazing on the actors playing the family who sit in limbo for long moments. Using a zoom lens to flatten the shot, Fassbinder pans across the faces of Emmi's two sons, her daughter and her son-in-law. Then her son Bruno whirls around in his chair, stands up and kicks in the screen of her TV set.

When Emmi introduces Ali to her family they sit in rows, ranked in gradations of dismay, staring, and the camera doesn't flinch, never cutting to the unconventional newly weds, insisting rather that we look at Emmi's offspring, whose racism spreads across their faces. The moment of artifice is broken and the reactions return to what we expect, names are called, threats are made, and Ali then comforts Emmi in her sorrow.

Mirrors are used in the film metonymically, for example where we see Emmi peer at herself in the mirror when she wakes after sleeping with Ali. She is clearly considering her age, and later when we again see Ali through a mirror in the shower we are reminded of the contrast by her comment, 'You are very handsome Ali'. This is said in a wistful tone which implies not desire for Ali but a desire to be young and attractive. These brief moments are rare glimpses of introspection; for much of the film we see only the public personas of the characters and very little of the private. This is highlighted later in the final bar scene where Ali is losing at cards and, he thinks, losing his relationship with Emmi. We see Ali impassively smack his own face in the mirror of the bar toilets. This highlights his personal crisis but also the makes us aware of how little we have seen of Ali alone.

sound and music

Fassbinder uses sound in conjunction with the mise-en-scène to complete the mannered effect in some of the tableau scenes. Thus, we hear the music from the jukebox in the bar and the sound of footsteps but the overall atmosphere is silence. Thus, we might well be puzzled later to find that the camera reveals many more people in the bar sitting near the dance area. Although not included in the earlier tableau of onlookers, their presence adds to the initial hostility with which Emmi is received, and the later acceptance.

audience aware of artifice

Much of the sound in the film is diegetic. One non-diegetic song crops up which was written by Fassbinder and signifies moments of tenderness. The Arab music from the jukebox is used to highlight the togetherness of the lovers and we see Emmi ask for it and select it herself. It does not appear by accident. Thus, music is rarely used to tell us what to feel, and this differs massively from Sirkian melodrama, where music is crucial to the raising and lowering of the emotional state of the audience.

the long shot: the long take

Employing a Sirkian stylisation in camera angle, framing, colour and lighting, Fassbinder takes on the conventions of melodrama in *Fear Eats the Soul*, yet exaggerates them in the direction of Bertolt Brecht. This emphasises the social type of the characters, arranging them in frozen tableaux at key moments, and distancing them by constantly framing through doorways and in long shot.

Ed Lowry, in The International Directory of Films and Filmmakers, 1997, p. 51

Fassbinder was motivated by the desire to make the audience aware of artifice and this he achieves in his use of the camera. He produces the sense of a stage set repeatedly at key moments within the film to bring the audience into focus on themselves as spectators not engaged in contemplation of the narrative.

In the opening bar scene, in each of the café scenes and in the infamous television scene, the setting becomes a stage set and the actors manikins. The camera keeps its distance for much longer than a traditional establishing shot, giving us only brief glimpses into the private world of the lovers. Throughout the film the editing follows the conventions of classic realist narrative film establishing logical and consequential action. His use of emphatic fade out after long takes separates the events and determines the passage of time. His intention is clearly to remind the audience that they are observers who are never able to see what the characters are thinking and feeling.

the long shot: the long take style

When Ali and Emmi are married they go to an expensive restaurant which Emmi points out was an old haunt of Hitler's. The interior is dark and the whole place is empty other than the two lovers and the waiter. The waiter is not revealed to us initially, but we sense he is there through Fassbinder's use of off-camera space. His gaze needless to say is disapproving. The lovers are shot in long distance through a doorway, which frames the scene. The decoration is dark blue and grey and thus cold; the lovers are dressed smartly but in a matching pale grey which seems at once nondescript and incongruous to their decision to marry. A huge classical landscape is the rather severe backdrop to their table. This is hardly the setting we might expect for a honeymoon meal.

The long takes at the beginning and end of the scene cut the lovers off from the world and the society which is about to stand in judgement over their decision to marry. It also serves as contrast to the dialogue once the camera finally allows us to move closer to Emmi and Ali. Now we are allowed our usual privileged access to the characters, and the acting shifts from mannered to naturalistic. Mira executes this scene brilliantly. Emmi is nervous but takes control of ordering from an expensive and unfamiliar menu. It is a moment which resonates, highlighting as it does the universal emotions of inadequacy and embarrassment which we are all subject to in unfamiliar social situations.

THE WAITER:

    Yes, madam? Are we ready to order?

EMMI:

    Yes, we're ready. Two cream of lobster soup.

    Two caviar. And one chateaubriand for two?

THE WAITER:

    How would you like your chateaubriand?

EMMI:

    How? Grilled I imagine.

WAITER:

    Quite so Madame. Grilled. But how? English or

    medium rare?

'Not raw is it?'

EMMI:

> What? English. That sounds fine.

WAITER:

> Right, English it is. Almost raw.

EMMI:

> Raw? (She looks at Ali for confirmation. He shakes his head) On second thoughts ...

WAITER:

> Yes madam?

EMMI:

> Raw, you say ... No I think we'd better – what was the other thing?

WAITER:

> Medium rare.

EMMI:

> That's right. Not raw is it?

WAITER:

> No, it's medium rare.

EMMI:

> Right. That sounds fine.

WAITER:

> And an aperitif to start with?

EMMI:

> A ...? Oh yes, of course.

WAITER:

> And what's it to be, madam?

EMMI:

> Well now, how about ... What do you recommend?

WAITER:

> The house aperitif, madam. I feel sure you'll like that.

the long shot: the long take style

symbolic of sexual attraction

EMMI:

> Right, if you say so ... Let's have that then.
> (*The waiter goes out. To Ali*) God, put me in a
> hell of a sweat, that did. Awful when you
> don't know what's what.

Ali's silence saves him from the overt gaze of the deeply offensive and aloof waiter – Emmi keeps him safe. In many ways it is a scene of great pathos. Although we are aware of Emmi's awkwardness and embarrassment, they seem happy and contented in their affection for each other. They do not allow the impenetrable and humourless waiter to ruin the occasion entirely. However, we don't witness them eating and drinking or indeed celebrating – we don't see joy. This ritual of enjoying a meal – which so often in film is symbolic of sexual attraction – is not included.

Later in the outdoor café these emotional responses are reinforced again throughout by the use of mise-en-scène, long shot and the creation of a small tableau of onlookers. The outdoor café should be a bright and vibrant location – the seats are all yellow and there is a park in the background, so we see trees and fields for the first time in the film. However, it is raining so despite being bright all the chairs and tables are empty, and we see Ali and Emmi isolated in the middle of the café. The camera moves very differently outside, panning more fluently around the table to take in both Ali and Emmi in close up. It reverts to a long shot of waiting staff and passers-by sheltering from the rain. They look on with blank faces, but Emmi reads this as contempt and this is the moment at which her strength breaks down. When Emmi bursts into tears the acting returns to a more naturalistic approach, and we engage strongly with Emmi's despair and Ali's attempts to comfort her.

ALI:

> Everybody inside looking.

EMMI:

> Take no notice. They're only envious.

ALI:

> Not understand envious.

'I just can't go on like this.'

EMMI:

If you're envious you can't stand seeing
another person with something you haven't
got.

ALI:

Right. Understand.

EMMI:

Envious, that's all they are. All of them.
(*She bursts into tears*) Every single one of
them.

ALI:

Why you crying?

EMMI:

Because ... Well, because in one way I'm
so happy, and then again I just can't go on
like this. The way everyone hates us.
Absolutely everybody. Wherever I go. I
sometimes wish I was completely alone with
you, and there was nobody else anywhere in
the world. Obviously I put a brave face on
the whole time, as if it didn't matter to
me, but it does matter to me, obviously.
It's just wearing me down. Nobody'll look me
in the eye anymore. People just grin in
that horrible way. Bastards. (*Shouting out*)
Bunch of bloody bastards! Stop gawping, you
stupid cretins! This is my husband, yes my
husband. (*In tears she puts her head in her
hands*)

ALI:

(*Stroking her hair*) Habibi. Habibi.

EMMI:

I love you, too.

the long shot: the long take style

ALI:

I more.

EMMI:

How much?

ALI:

This much. (Spreading out his arms)

Emmi:

And I love you from here to Morocco. I'll tell
you what. We'll go on holiday. Somewhere away
from it all. Somewhere nobody knows us and
nobody gawps at us. And by the time we get
back everything will have changed. And
everybody will be really nice to us. You mark
my words. (Blackout)

Ali's simple responses to Emmi's distress are poignant but affirm the simplicity of their relationship. He cheers her with a child-like game of who loves whom more. It is again Emmi who not only articulates her own anger and sorrow but also proposes a solution, which although unconvincing somehow proves to be true. When they return from their holiday they are more accepted by their society, but this is motivated by compromise rather than any changes of heart (see Narrative & Form: Theme).

framing

Fassbinder's use of framing has been described as 'obtrusively stylised' (Watson, 1992, p. 24), by which it is meant that we notice it. Fassbinder does not intend us to notice the framing out of an appreciation of the aesthetic of the shot; however, he wishes the audience to be aware of where the camera is positioned in relation to the world of the film. He also seeks to use the structures that are available to him to create the sense of the characters being observed, not only by the judgmental neighbours but also the audience. The camera observes the moments when characters interact through lattice meshes and stair arches, and the experience of watching at these moments is not to be drawn in but to be repelled, to feel outside – even closed out. This can be illustrated particularly with reference to the exterior shots, all of which are virtually empty streets that have a 'Sunday in a city' feel to them. They are also predominantly grey and flat, and are shot from and through doorways and windows. These shapes are held in the outer reaches of the shot so that the camera becomes the observer and Fassbinder creates the sense of surveillance: the lovers are observed and judged.

When Emmi goes to the local shop to complain about Ali's treatment we see her return through an open door. It is not revealed who is looking from the doorway but it is implied that it is one of the many disapproving neighbours. There are parallel scenes that take place in the stairwells and corridors of the apartment buildings. Here we see chipped and damp paintwork and greys and whites that again give an empty cold feel. These passages belong to no one. Yet they are the point at which neighbours and fellow cleaners meet, and are therefore where Emmi receives the punishing comments and judgements about her relationship with Ali.

The framing of these scenes makes use of the many angles created by the staircase ascent and the presence of lattice grilles and banisters through which characters are shot. For example we see Emmi sitting eating her lunch as she has done before on the stairs with her workmates. They have now discovered her relationship with Ali and they coldly ignore her presence.

The final shot of this scene is taken through the banister, where we see Emmi slowly and deliberately eating her lunch at some distance above her condemning colleagues. We have seen her earlier in exactly the same place eating her lunch whilst chatting with them. Later we see a parallel shot of Jolanda, a new immigrant worker ignored by the others who now accept Emmi back into the group. This parallel reminds us of Emmi's initial isolation and confronts us with her lack of compassion towards one now in a similar position. The stairwells in the apartment building where Emmi lives are equally the site of her initial rejection and then reconciliation with her neighbours.

framing

foregrounds Emmi's alienation

A conversation through a lattice,
this scene foregrounds Emmi's
alienation from friends and
neighbours

FEAR EATS THE SOUL

dialogue

Like many of the New German Cinema directors Fassbinder often dispensed with a scriptwriter. He wrote the script for the film himself, retaining the simple story, which he liked and he felt gave the film universal appeal. Thus, the dialogue is itself simple and contains few extended speeches. Ali speaks in good but not always grammatically perfect German. In public situations Emmi does the talking. However, the simplicity with which they communicate with each other is used to good effect.

On the evening following their first night together Emmi seeks Ali in the bar where the atmosphere towards her is now entirely hostile. She leaves only to find Ali waiting for her outside the apartment building. She is clearly delighted and they say very little:

EMMI:

    Ali.

ALI:

    Good to see you.

EMMI:

    Yes, well.

ALI:

    Yes.

EMMI:

    Right, then.

This interchange unfortunately loses something in the translation. When they exchange the word 'ja' they exchange a promise signalled in their visual contact. They are making a commitment to each other; they understand each other. More dialogue than this is not necessary.

contexts

genre: melodrama

And I don't believe that melodramatic feelings are laughable – they
should be taken absolutely seriously.

Fassbinder, quoted in Sight and Sound, Vol. 44, No. 1, Winter 74/75, p. 3

Fassbinder made films which utilised the generic expectations of his
audience. It is important to recognise that the usefulness of the concept of
genre goes well beyond that of a typology. In fact, many Film Studies
theorists have pointed to the inadequacy of genre study which only
focuses on defining a set of rules by which each genre abides.

Film genres have developed not as clear and distinct bodies of work
with consistent things in common, but as dynamic and evolving groups of
films, which might also overlap from one group to another. For example,
the 'romance' genre overlaps with 'romance comedy', and indeed might
yield to further demarcation as sub-genres such as the 'screwball comedy'.
Some genres are more powerful than others; they differ in the status,
which is attributed to them by those who make them, and by their
audiences.

Fassbinder's approach to using melodrama developed considerably
after *Fear Eats the Soul*; however, the common element to all his
melodramas is his conscious manipulation of the generic expectations
of the audience (see Style). It is important to establish the way in which
the term melodrama has developed in relation to film and film audiences.
There are a large number of groups of films which have been defined
under this heading. In Thomas and Vivian Sobchack's taxonomy of film
genres (Sobchack, Thomas and Vivien C., 1980, p. 245), a basic distinction
is made (beyond whether a text is fiction or non-fiction) between comedy
and melodrama.

FEAR EATS THE SOUL

genre: melodrama

The Sobchacks list the main genres of comedy as: slapstick comedy; romantic comedy, including screwball comedy and musical comedy; musical biography; and fairytale. They list the main genres of melodrama as: adventure films, including 'the swashbuckler' and 'survival films' (the war movie, the safari film, and disaster movies); the western; 'fantastic genres', including fantasy, horror and science fiction; and 'antisocial genres', including the crime film (the gangster film, the G-man film, the private eye or detective film, the film noir, the caper film) and so-called 'weepies' (or 'women's films').

This use of melodrama as a broad-brush expression to include a range of genres is quite different to the way the term has been used to discuss certain film genres within that list – that is to say 'weepies', 'sudsers' or 'women's films'. All three terms have been used variously by the industry and audiences to refer to a group of films which place a female character at the centre, are thematically linked by issues of morality and position in society, and are home focused.

These films were also often dominated by the concept of fortune and coincidence – impossible love stories between ill-matched partners. These terms have been used as derogatory and demeaning frames of reference for a genre that has been perceived as lower status than others such as 'the western' or 'the gangster movie'. Audiences and industry used the term to refer to particular films which were 'overemotional'. The word was used in the way we might use the term 'drama queen' today to refer to an over-the-top emotional state.

Film Studies largely ignored the melodrama genre, perhaps viewing it as cynical and exploitative of female audience without investigating what pleasures were on offer to the audience and how the audience elicited meanings. This is a common perspective typified by those Marxist commentators who see genre as an instrument of social control which reproduces the dominant ideology. Genre hierarchies, however, shift over time, with individual genres 'constantly gaining and losing different groups of users and relative status' (Daniel Chandler, 1997, www document).

Study of the melodrama as a cinematic genre is a recent development still in its early stages. It achieved public visibility in

> 1977 when the Society for Education in Film and Television commissioned papers for a study weekend, some of which were subsequently published in *Screen and Movie* in the UK and the *Australian Journal of Film Theory*. Around this time and since a spate of articles have appeared in British, French and American film journals and interest in the genre has been extended to work on television, particularly soap operas.
>
> *Pam Cook (ed.), 1985, p. 73*

Melodrama was championed in the 1970s in the world of Film Studies, as for example in Laura Mulvey's review of *Fear Eats the Soul*, which appeared in *Spare Rib*, a feminist publication, in 1974. Her review argued a feminist interest in the genre.

> Mulvey begins to show how melodrama can function for patriarchal ends, bringing about a narrative resolution of its contradictions, and at the same time perform a quite different function for women: offering the satisfaction of recognising those contradictory needs.
>
> *ibid, p. 77*

Daniel Chandler highlights the neglect within genre theory of the audience: 'Practitioners and the general public make use of their own genre labels (de facto genres) quite apart from those of academic theorists ... If we are studying the way in which genre frames the reader's interpretation of a text then we would do well to focus on how readers identify genres rather than on theoretical distinctions' (1997, www document). Certainly this can be argued in the case of melodrama, where studies initially focused on authorship. Mulvey's work signalled a fresh approach which also accounted for audiences' pleasure. Fassbinder is a film maker who recognised the need to address the tacit contract between authors and readers.

In melodrama the narrative often centres on a series of decisions which involve the protagonist in choosing between family and her own personal needs. The obstacles which arise disrupt the status quo of the family, which

genre: melodrama

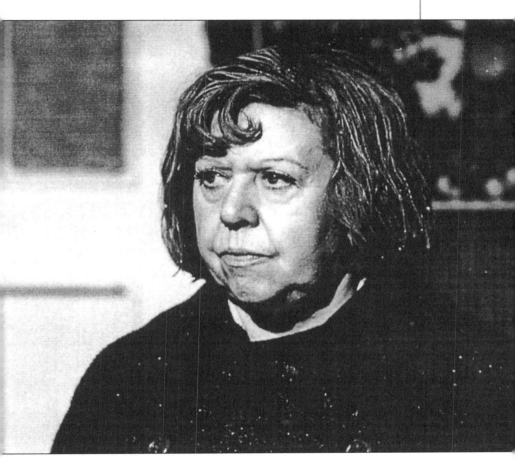

Emmi, the central character,
suffers angst in her desire
for acceptance

suffers great angst

is the dominant location of Hollywood melodrama, that is to say the middle-class white family home. This space is closed and confined, and structures the action into that sometimes claustrophobic space of the home. The intensity in the atmosphere is reflected in the appearance of the interior of this home, an artificially smooth surface beneath which bubbles the tension and repressed hysteria of the central character.

The narrative is often driven by the decision-making of this central character, who is faced with some kind of personal struggle and who suffers great angst and dilemmas over personal sacrifice. There are often peripheral characters looking in from the outside who sit in judgement of the main character, representing the values of society. Typical themes explored are the struggle for personal freedom and individuality against a backdrop of the family representing society. Repression, particularly in relation to sexual relationships, is reflected through clever use of mise-en-scène. The home is affluent and use of colour is vibrant, often contrasting with the coldness and lack of emotion expressed by the family (see Narrative & Form: Narrative).

Fassbinder's use of melodrama coincides with a period when New German Film makers were the subject of criticism for films which were inaccessible and did not reach the audience. At the same time there were debates within the state-funding regime about the ways in which documentary should be clearly distinguishable from fiction. Fassbinder employed melodramatic structure and mise-en-scène but also a style which emphasised the fictional nature of his work (see Style).

filmography: fassbinder and sirk

Sirk's is a kind of fairytale: mine too, but one from everyday life. Sirk had the courage simply to tell the story. I probably didn't trust myself simply to do that.

Fassbinder, quoted in Sight and Sound, Vol. 44, No. 1, Winter 74/75, p. 2

The links between *Fear Eats the Soul* and *All That Heaven Allows* have been clearly established elsewhere in these notes. However, it is worth

filmography

contemplating Fassbinder's interpretation of Sirk's films, which were to have such an impact on his own work.

In his understanding of the audience's relationship with genre it could be argued that Fassbinder was ahead of the game. He read *All That Heaven Allows* as subversive rather than conservative. Thomas and Vivian Sobchack note that in the past popular film-makers 'intent on telling a story' were not always aware of 'the covert psychological and social ... subtext' of their own films, but add that modern film makers and their audiences are now 'more keenly aware of the myth making accomplished by film genres' (Sobchack, Thomas and Vivien C., 1980, p. 245).

Fassbinder certainly believed this was true of Sirk and that he accomplished his art in under difficult circumstances. 'To Sirk something still mattered that most people in Hollywood don't care about anymore: making his work in tune with his own personality, that is not just produced for the public' (Fassbinder, quoted in Watson, 1996, p. 4).

German-trained Douglas Sirk made *Written on the Wind, All That Heaven Allows, Magnificent Obsession* and *Imitation of Life* for Universal Pictures during the 1950s. Fassbinder was attracted to these films not only for their entertainment value but also for their representation of various kinds of exploitation.

'The model of Sirk's highly crafted but critical melodramas of American life in the 1950's inspired and helped Fassbinder as he sought now to move beyond what he already considered his apprentice period' (ibid.). He wanted to make German Hollywood films – he had a strong desire for his films to reach an audience.

The differences between Fassbinder and Sirk are more obvious the closer their subject is. In *All That Heaven Allows* an accident befalls Rock Hudson, and this is the action which reunites the lovers. In *Fear Eats the Soul* the lovers reunite because Emmi seeks out Ali after their argument. They forgive each other the wrongs they have done but Ali is struck down by an illness which we later learn is common to immigrant workers and is caused by stress. Fassbinder does not allow the audience the easy option of an accidental or coincidental device – he asks them to consider the causes.

production: fassbinder's studio system

> But when he worked with the camera and with actors he had the grace and vitality of a ballet dancer.
>
> *Braad Thomsen, 1997, p. 1*

Fassbinder's reputation as a film maker reflects some interesting contradictions. Firstly, he was well known for surrounding himself with a familiar cast and crew that he often had a close personal relationship with. This style of working was perhaps influenced by his involvement in the theatre where the same company would work together on a range of projects. However, it should not be inferred that Fassbinder had a democratic style of leadership nor that his film projects were the result of collaborative efforts.

> The greatest tension one sensed in Fassbinder was probably the contradiction between constant attempts to realise his dream of a productive community, and the aggressive atmosphere that surrounded him and which he usually created himself. Whenever he turned up, there were quarrels, crises, explosions.
>
> *ibid.*

Fassbinder claimed that he used the same group of actors in his company because the possibilities for agreement were so much better. His use of familiar personnel was certainly pragmatic as they became accustomed to his way of working and each project was not like starting anew. He also expressed concerns about the low budget he had available to pay staff and this impacted on his working practice. Shoots were swift and intensive and he rarely spent time on one particular take.

Hollywood studio directors Walsh, Curtiz and Sirk are nostalgically described by Fassbinder as lone individuals in a regimented system of studio rules, where creativity was the poor relation of commercial success. Fassbinder was fascinated by those systems and recognised what was

production

successful in the way Hollywood studios organised production: keeping to deadlines and working with crew who built up knowledge of the director's style and understood his vision. These were, again, pragmatic working structures which Fassbinder mirrored in his own productions.

In all of his early work and in particular in *Fear Eats the Soul*, Fassbinder was working on a small budget. State funding was insufficient and this influenced the non-commercial look of many of the films of New German Cinema. Thus, Fassbinder was maximising available human resources to compensate for what he lacked in production time. The constraints he worked within were simply different to those of the US studios. However, his fast-expanding body of work and reputation for on-schedule delivery soon meant that Fassbinder was given autonomy over the content of his films. This results in an interesting assessment of Fassbinder's body of work:

> Fassbinder was an unusually disciplined and sure-handed director, who carefully sketched out most of his shots in advance. And he worked fast, typically omitting rehearsals and going with his first take. The result is that though his total body of work is rich in cinematic texture and form, not one of his films is quite a perfect masterpiece.
>
> *Wallace Watson, Sight and Sound, June 1992, p. 24*

Fassbinder the director was an autocrat. He worked his actors hard and manipulated them using the personal ties he held with them. Fassbinder has been described as cruel and harsh on set. Indeed, parallels could be drawn with Hitchcock, who, like Fassbinder, was well known for his emotional cruelty towards female actors.

> Anyone who sees Fassbinder films senses immediately that they are made by an extremely strong dictatorial personality. But he did not give the actors an intellectual explanation of what he had in mind. He transmitted it indirectly, through the particular atmosphere he created during filming. Irm Herman once described how during the making of *Berlin Alexanderplatz*, Fassbinder had suddenly begun to make fun of her in front of everyone, until she

> broke down crying. At that moment, Fassbinder gave the
> cameraman a signal and asked Irm to play the scene which she did
> to his complete satisfaction.
>
> *Braad Thomsen, 1997, p. 30*

Accounts of this harsh treatment form the baptise of several less than
insightful biographical kiss and tell accounts of Fassbinder's life and work.
Often these retain the personal tensions between the writer and the film
maker. Braad Thomsen's account, based on many interviews with actors
and crew, offers an insight into the loyalty that Fassbinder inspired in spite
of his dictatorial approach. He argues that Fassbinder dominated his actors
and bullied them to achieve the performances he required. Although many
were loyal at the time they now acknowledge this brutal way of working
and the lack of any direct verbal communication between themselves and
the director.

> When he comes to the shoots, he always knows exactly how the
> takes should look: you can call that dictatorial, but it's agreeable
> compared to directors who don't know what they want when the
> camera is standing there and the lights are on. Rainer knows
> everything before he does it and that gives everyone a sense of
> security. That's why everything can happen so fast, because he
> always arrives with this conviction about how it should be.
>
> *Irm Herman, quoted in Braad Thomsen, 1997, p. 9*

Despite this autocratic reality, Fassbinder held on to a more utopian vision
of the film set as an extended family where for a time everyone lived
together and worked together. This is played out in a number of films. He
came close to this vision on the set for *Chinese Roulette* where each night
he made everyone play Chinese roulette, a psychological truth game, and
this resulted in fits of hysteria and tears. However, during the day the
work continued. Christien Braad Thomsen argues that this method was an
inherent part of the way Fassbinder elicited such good performances from
his actors.

In *Fear Eats the Soul*, it could be argued that Fassbinder is trying to avert
these tensions. Although the film was made quickly and in a typically

new german cinema

intensive manner, Fassbinder chose a lead character with whom he had not established an intense personal relationship. When asked in interview about the casting of Brigitte Mira – a formerly well-known actress whose prominence had declined – he commented 'I simply found myself longing for people who come in return for pay, do decent work and don't torment me'. He describes Mira as pragmatic and down-to-earth; a person who works for pay in a profession usually more associated with artistic purpose.

Fassbinder also uses Salem's relative lack of experience as an actor to keep the simplicity of the character. By giving his lover the leading role he is already promoting him well above the bit parts that he was used to playing. Although *Fear Eats the Soul* is in many ways typical of Fassbinder's production practices, there are some important differences in the way he relates to and works with the actors chosen for the lead roles. Fassbinder clearly hoped for a certain amount of docility or acquiescence from the lead characters. Unusually Fassbinder made as many as twenty takes of some shots despite the lack of time, and this is reflected in the performances, which despite the minimal dialogue and acting style are warm and engaging.

Fassbinder says of Mira and Salem 'I never worked with film actors the way I worked with those two. I really wanted to get the maximum out of every moment'. Thus he found himself able to be creative with actors who were not being wound up to emotional heights and this again leads to performances which are accessible to a wider audience in their quiet sorrow and desperate yearnings. They are more representative of the audience's expectations of lovers than some alternatives in Fassbinder's work.

new german cinema

I now think the primary need is to satisfy the audience, and then to deal with political content. First, you have to make films that are seductive, beautiful, about emotion.

Fassbinder, quoted in Sight and Sound, Vol. 44, No. 1, Winter 74/75, p. 2

Fassbinder was the best-known member of a group of second generation, alternative film makers in West Germany. Although he used the idea of a new cinema to promote his work, he also remained distinct because of his attitude to his audience, which was greatly influenced by mainstream Hollywood and the predominance of his personal life. The first generation of film makers consisted of Alexander Kluge and others who in 1962 drafted the *Oberhausen Manifesto*, initiating what has come to be called the New German Cinema. This non-commercial West German cinema of the 1960s and 1970s was both aesthetically eclectic and politically radical – markedly different from other film movements such as Italian Neo Realist and French New Wave because of the absence of a unifying style.

After the occupation of Germany following the Second World War, America was one of the occupying forces. American cinema dominated, and this was seen unproblematically at first as the need to educate through entertainment. German audiences were to be de-Nazified through film narratives, which sought to demonstrate the error of their ways.

With the rise of the Cold War, American anti-communist policies led to the dominance of the industry by directors and crews from the political right, who often had Nazi backgrounds. West German post-war cinema largely consisted of pastoral romances and apologetic war films. Simultaneously faced with the expansion of television, the native film industry of the 1960s was impoverished and 'on the brink of collapse'. These factors led the West German government to welcome the *Oberhausen Manifesto* of 1962, in which a collection of young German film makers argued for a subsidised non-commercial cinema.

THE OBERHAUSEN MANIFESTO (1962)

The collapse of the conventional German film finally removes the economic basis for a mode of filmmaking whose attitude and practice we reject. With it the new film has a chance to come to life. German short films by young authors, directors, and producers have in recent years received a large number of prizes at international festivals and gained the recognition of international critics. These works and these successes show that the future of the German film lies in the hands of those who have proven that they speak a new film language. Just as in other countries, the short film has become in Germany, a school and experimental basis for the feature film. We declare our intention to create the new German feature film. This new film needs new freedoms:

Freedom from the conventions of the established industry. Freedom from the outside influence of commercial partners. Freedom from the control of special interest groups.

We have concrete intellectual, formal, and economic conceptions about the production of the new German film. We are as a collective prepared to take economic risks. The old film is dead. We believe in the new one.

Oberhausen, February 28, 1962

The first films made within this system have became known as Young German Cinema and include Alexander Kluge's *Abschied von Gestern* [Yesterday Girl] (1966), Edbar Reitz's *Mahlzeiten* [Meal Times] and Daniele Huillet and Jean Marie Straub's *Nict Verssohnt* [Not Reconciled] (1965). Although these films vary in theme, they are typified by a narrative and formal austerity and the fact that they were largely ignored by audiences.

However, they paved the way for a new generation of film makers including Herzog and Fassbinder who produced their first features in 1968 (*Lebenszeichen*) and in 1969 (*Love is Colder than Death*) respectively. These films were made at a time of political upheaval including the 1968 student rebellions, the anti-American protests in relation to the Vietnam war, and an emergence of a distinct youth culture which included massive music festivals and the use of psychedelic drugs.

State funding relationships with film makers created a situation where films which catechised the state could be made. These films, which were often exhibited abroad by the Goethe Institute, also served as an exercise in public relations for the West German government who were seen to be able to accept criticism. The audiences for these films in Germany itself were largely students politicised by the events of 1968. They did not reach mass audiences, and were likely to be screened at Trade Union meetings or feminist conferences rather than cinemas.

German television networks also played a crucial role in feature film production. Funding from co-productions with television enabled the director to retain rights to a film for theatrical exhibition. Once established with the television networks the film maker retained autonomy over individual works. Certainly television commissions enabled Fassbinder to be prolific and explore the medium of television.

Thematically, the films were linked by a preoccupation with the concept of national identity and the influences of the recent past, although these were not necessarily dealt with explicitly. Formally, there were fewer links although David Bordwell (1985, pp. 206–7) identifies, 'ambling narratives with a lingering on details and seemingly unimportant events: a stress on mood rather than actions and an overall sense of ambiguity'.

The lack of a unifying style in New German Cinema can be seen as a reaction against the cultural domination of both Nazism and Hollywood:

> The directors' rejection of German commercial film was manifested in their refusal to follow established German film genre and in their reluctance to hire well known German stars or create their own. The (mediated) influence of American narrative conventions is more noticeable than any continuity with German cinema.
>
> Sieglohr in Hill and Church Gibson (eds), 1998, p. 66

Wim Wender's *Kings of the Road* and *Hammett* refer to American road movies and film noir respectively, just as Fassbinder refers to the melodrama of Sirk. This is where Fassbinder departs from his fellow film makers in a mission to widen his audience. Fassbinder is distinctive within this group because of his overt desire to combine the traditions of Hollywood cinema, particularly Hollywood realist narrative, and the politics of this new cinema movement. However, some shared themes with his contemporaries Kluge, Straub and Huillet can be identified. Many concentrate on disadvantaged social groups or outsiders, especially people from lower- or middle-class backgrounds.

fassbinder's audience

New German directors considered themselves the sole authors of their work, taking on the script writing and producing themselves. Thus, the directors of the New German Cinema themselves became a key marketing tool for promoting the films and the concept of New German Cinema. Elsaesser argues that New German Cinema gained recognition only after the acclaim it received abroad, which was courted by the film makers. This is particularly true of Fassbinder (see Background: Director as Auteur).

The early 1980s (shortly after Fassbinder's death) mark the end of this period of German cinema, when individual film makers took very different directions, many taking up International projects.

fassbinder's audience: in the distance

And if art, or whatever you want to call it, seizes the opportunity to get discussion going among people, it's achieved its maximum effect.

Fassbinder, quoted in Toteberg and Lensing (eds), 1992, p. 12

Fassbinder's current status as an auteur stems from his unique relationship with the audience. His work moved outside the boundaries of both 'Art House' and mainstream film, and included gangster films, melodrama and film noir. He was consistently engaged with evoking responses from the audience, and this has a huge and recognisable impact on his style. *Fear Eats the Soul* is particularly effective because although he uses a popular genre, melodrama, he transports the story out of the bourgeois settings of Hollywood melodrama. He infuses the film with devices, which force the audience to reflect on their familiarity with that genre.

Arranging characters in frozen tableaux at key moments and distancing the viewer by constantly framing through doorways and in long shot.

Ed Lowry, in The International Dictionary of Films and Filmmakers, 1997, p. 51

active in their interpretation

Despite the settings of his films Fassbinder was not a social realist, though many of his narratives would have fitted this style and structure. Instead of trying to get as close as possible to the characters, creating authenticity, he opts for the illusion of distance. *Fear Eats the Soul* opens just like a stage set and establishes characters whose actions appear mechanised. The camera's position at the centre of the bar, reversing from one side to the other, gives an almost tableau-like feel as if each character was simply a part of the mise-en-scène of the room. Indeed there are moments in this scene where the camera movement reveals more people drinking in the bar, whose silence throughout the opening five minutes adds to the feeling that this was a carefully planned mime-like performance. Fassbinder attempts to distance the audience 'in favour of their own reality'.

> At some point films have to stop being films, being stories, and have to begin to come alive so that people will ask themselves: What about me and my life?
>
> *Fassbinder, quoted in Toteberg and Lensing (eds), 1992, p. 11*

Fassbinder was torn between the contradictory belief that people do not change yet they could be made aware of things. 'Since I'm not a second Marx or Freud who can offer people alternatives, I have to let them keep their own wrong feelings' (Fassbinder).

He wanted his films to act on people – to force them to be active in their interpretation. This is particularly true during the period in which he made *Fear Eats the Soul*. Fassbinder never subscribed to the ever-popular view that people are fundamentally incapable of actively interpreting media. Indeed, in his attitude towards his audience, which is staked out throughout the creative process of his film making, his own considerable faith in people's desire to be challenged is revealed. Having said this, his own attraction to the work of certain Hollywood directors, coupled with his intuitive understanding of the pleasures elicited by mainstream genre films, meant that his work emerged in a particular direction. He talked of 'seduction' and of 'meeting the entertainment factor half way'. *Fear Eats the Soul* was made at a time when these ideas were still comparatively new to Fassbinder and thus the film is explorative.

fassbinder's audience

Later films such as *Lola, Veronica Voss* and *The Marriage of Maria Braun* make more sophisticated use of the conventions and structures of melodrama to convey more complex ideas about Germany after the Second World War. We are privileged today to have access to Fassbinder's emerging ideas about audience and genre, which give us a great insight into the decisions he makes about the style and structure of the film.

> Sirk told me what the studio bosses in Hollywood told him: a film has to go over in Okinawa, and in Chicago – just try to think what the common denominator might be for people in all those places.
>
> *ibid, p. 12*

Fassbinder's recollection of this comment reveals his motivation to produce a film about universal themes, and explains his determination to keep the story and the characters simple. Although the film did reach a much wider and international audience than earlier work, it must be acknowledged that this was still not a mass audience in comparison with mainstream Hollywood, and that his films played the 'Art House' circuit. Fassbinder received some criticism that his films were sentimental (see Critical Responses) largely because the audiences were made up of the educated middle classes.

The accusation of sentimentality reflects the widely held derogatory light in which melodrama is held – spoken of as soap opera continues to be today. However, Fassbinder had no reservations about using emotion and placing his characters in desperate and hostile situations. It is questionable whether *Fear Eats the Soul* can be accused of sentimentality, refraining as it does from scenes of tender expression or private love. The film also avoids the sound and camera conventions so often used in melodrama to signify peaks of emotion. This again points to the way in which Fassbinder attempts to elicit an audience response but is equally determined to ensure that that response is one which stems from the spectator's own experience of the themes within the story.

Not only does Fassbinder want to reach the audience, he wants them to be active participants in their reading of the film: 'to dissociate themselves

simultaneously subverting them

from the story, not at the expense of the film but rather in favour of their
own reality' (ibid.).

> The peculiar flavour of his achievement is to alienate us and
> involve us at the same time.
>
> *Andy Medhurst, Sight and Sound, Feb 1996, p. 22*

critical responses

During Fassbinder's lifetime his work was more enthusiastically received
abroad than it was at home. At home he was better known for his
controversial lifestyle than his films. His disregard for political correctness
was controversial – he was vilified by the left and right, accused of
misogyny by feminists, and even anti-Semitism. Fassbinder's name was
frequently in the papers, bitterly denouncing his country: 'Better a street-
sweeper in Mexico than a film maker in Germany!'

A large number of retrospectives of Fassbinder's work have taken place both
in his lifetime in Paris, London and New York, and posthumously, including
one at the NFT in 1999 which went on to tour independent cinemas across
the UK. The Goethe Institute and other institutions promoting German
culture have funded these tours and events. It may strike some as ironic
that Fassbinder is celebrated as a national asset, he 'whose personal life
and artistic production so insistently challenged German mainstream
culture' (Wallace Watson, *Sight and Sound*, June 1992, p. 24).

Perhaps it is more relevant to reflect on the political and cultural changes
which force us to look at Fassbinder's work outside its cultural specificity.
The political climate has moved on so far that what seemed outrageous
now seems pertinent. His critics contend that he became so infatuated
with the Hollywood forms he tried to appropriate that the political impact
of his films is indistinguishable from conventional melodrama, while his
admirers argue that he was a postmodernist film maker whose films satisfy
audience expectations whilst simultaneously subverting them.

In this review of critical responses to his work there emerges a repeated
fascination with the life of the man and what he might mean for audiences
today.

critical responses

Fassbinder produced an entirely original oeuvre that remains as imaginative today as it did when he was alive. But when he was alive the extent of his achievement was obscured. Accessibility to his work was limited due to the vagaries of foreign (outside Germany that is) film distribution. His work, being radical, suffered the shock and bewilderment that always greets the new. The media folderol that attended his life also denigrated his talent. He was one of, if not, the first internationally known filmmakers who was not embarrassed to be thought of as homosexual. He was often photographed in a leather jacket, defiant and unkempt: this image stood for the man, and this trite representation constantly intruded upon critical judgements of his work.

Larry Kardish, National Film Theatre programme Jan / Feb 1999 – RWF retrospective

This introduction is typical of the way Fassbinder is presented as both an auteur and a star. It also denies his complicity with the development of his own image. Kardish goes on to praise 'his essential empathy, his ability to unsettle convention, replacing it with illuminating insight, his passion for honesty [which] made him an ironic chronicler of contemporary Germany'.

A mammoth retrospective by Manhattan's Museum of Modern Art, also curated by Kurdish, at which all 43 of Fassbinder's films were screened, paid tribute to 'the career of Rainer Werner Fassbinder, Germany's most famous post-war filmmaker ... A titan of '70s cinema'.

What appeals to younger audiences today is the man's honesty and his films' simplicity. They're the antithesis of the MTV type of filmmaking we see today. One learns through his films a great deal about a country putting itself back together after the war.

Andy Medhurst, Sight and Sound, Feb 1996, p. 22

Fassbinder's movies are rebellious, stylised, and theatrical, unlike anyone else's. Like Andy Warhol, Fassbinder celebrated those at society's edge: drag queens, drug addicts, minorities, the depressed or suicidal. Indeed, Fassbinder's life prefigured themes that have dominated American life in the past 20 years: bisexuality, drug use, an incredible work ethic and self-destruction.

ibid.

This is typical of the sort of eulogy which Fassbinder's work, life and death elicited and which Elsaesser refers to in his introduction to the NFT's 'Fassbinder Lives' conference:

> When Fassbinder died in 1982, critics outside Germany eulogised him as the chief representative, not only of the New German Cinema but of a new Germany. A surprising turn of events, one might think, since the idea of Fassbinder standing for more that his own uniquely idiosyncratic world is inherently implausible. And yet, the intervening years, with such no less unexpected turn of events as the fall of the wall oblige one to rethink the place of Fassbinder's films. By standing up against much that the old federal republic stood for, they are proving retrospectively prophetic and emerge as a factor in forcing Germans to rethink their present in order to live with their history
>
> *Thomas Elsaesser, 1999*

What links these views is the emphasis on the continuing resonance for contemporary audiences which Fassbinder's work offers. He is presented as ahead of his time, dealing with contemporary issues and offering a representation of Germany which uniquely reflects upon its recent past.

> Fassbinder's films probe relentlessly beneath the repressed surfaces of individual lives and the deceptive 'normality' of modern social and political arrangements, to reveal oppression and exploitation in many forms in both personal and public spheres.
>
> *Wallace Watson, Sight and Sound, June 1992, p. 24*

It should not be assumed that Fassbinder was ever universally positively received, as this review of *Fear Eats the Soul* demonstrates:

> As the first of Fassbinder's films to receive a release in this country, *Fear Eats the Soul* has been rather disproportionately heaped with

critical responses

critical praises – which also seem to have been denied release for too long. Not the best of the director's recent films, it is the supple cunning with which he tells a quasi realistic tale of love's labour frustrated by social prejudice within a stylised format which gives the cultural confrontation between the lonely German char the doleful Moroccan immigrant peculiar gravity and destiny.

Richard Combs, Monthly Film Bulletin, Nov 1974, p. 244

Indeed a review of all of Fassbinder's work produced shortly after his death accuses him of sentimentality:

If I had to define the puzzling mixture of ingredients that typically make up a Fassbinder film I would say it was one part loutish truculence, one part intellectual toughness and one part treacly sentimentality ... What is problematic is that Fassbinder's populism may be the worst kind of compromise, aiming at a kind of embourgeoisement where everyone is allowed the luxury of self pity. ... Fear Eats the Soul strikes one as an even 'sudsier' soap opera, a real 'tear-jerker' to knee-jerk Liberals.

James Roy MacBean, Sight and Sound, Vol. 52, No. 1, Winter 82/83, p. 42

Whilst it is possible to reason that this view of the film reflects an overall negative attitude to melodrama (see Genre) it is interesting that the film in which Fassbinder unusually adapts the ending to give a positive outlook is the most catechised. Much more typical of contemporary responses are the following:

Fassbinder's fifteenth film *Angst essen Seele auf*, represents perhaps the peak of his renowned domestic melodrama period, bracketed approximately by *The Merchant of the Four seasons* and *Angst von Angst.*

Ed Lowry, in The International Directory of Films and Filmmakers, 1997, p. 51

Both *Fox* and *Fear Eats the Soul* are at once exact diagrams of particular structures of oppression, and gut-wrenching stories inviting real empathy. Two sensibilities, the diagnostic and the melodramatic feeding off each other in an uneasy and compelling co-existence, held together yet kept apart by the formal play of the films.

Andy Medhurst, Sight and Sound, Feb 1996, p. 22

As has been discussed throughout this review, Fassbinder's life penetrates interpretations of his work both with his audiences during his lifetime and with film academics now. Much has been written of his duality – his life and work – which are full of contradictions.

Fassbinder's very real achievement as a filmmaker lies in his ability to walk a tightrope of paradoxes (and contradiction) stretched to the breaking point by the cruel twists of his own masochistic but none the less demanding logic.

James Roy Macbean, Sight and Sound, Vol. 52, No. 1, Winter 82/83, p. 42

The duality of Fassbinder's nature is at the heart of the writings of Christian Braad Thomsen whose intimacy with both Fassbinder and his work enable him to write about both with knowledge and insight.

bibliography

general film

Altman, Rick, *Film Genre*,
BFI, 1999
Detailed exploration of film genres

Bordwell, David, *Narration in the
Fiction Film*, Routledge, 1985
A detailed study of narrative theory
and structures

– – –, Staiger, Janet & Thompson,
Kristin, *The Classical Hollywood
Cinema: Film Style & Mode of
Production to 1960*, Routledge, 1985;
pbk 1995
An authoritative study of cinema as
institution, it covers film style and
production

– – – & Thompson, Kristin, *Film Art*,
McGraw-Hill, 4th edn, 1993
An introduction to film aesthetics for
the non-specialist

Branson, Gill & Stafford, Roy, *The
Media Studies Handbook*, Routledge,
1996

Buckland, Warren, *Teach Yourself
Film Studies*, Hodder & Stoughton,
1998
Very accessible, it gives an overview
of key areas in film studies

Cook, Pam (ed.), *The Cinema Book*,
BFI, 1994

Corrigan, Tim, *A Short Guide To
Writing About Film*,
HarperCollins, 1994
What it says: a practical guide for
students

Dyer, Richard, *Stars*, BFI, 1979;
pbk Indiana University Press, 1998
A good introduction to the star
system

Easthope, Antony, *Classical Film
Theory*, Longman, 1993
A clear overview of recent writing
about film theory

Hayward, Susan, *Key Concepts in
Cinema Studies*,
Routledge, 1996

Hill, John & Gibson, Pamela Church
(eds), *The Oxford Guide to Film Studies*,
Oxford University Press, 1998
Wide-ranging standard guide

Lapsley, Robert & Westlake, Michael,
Film Theory: An Introduction,
Manchester University Press, 1994

Maltby, Richard & Craven, Ian,
Hollywood Cinema,
Blackwell, 1995
A comprehensive work on the
Hollywood industry and its
products

Mulvey, Laura, 'Visual Pleasure and
Narrative Cinema' (1974), in *Visual
and Other Pleasures*,
Indiana University Press, Bloomington,
1989
The classic analysis of 'the look' and
'the male gaze' in Hollywood cinema.
Also available in numerous other
edited collections

Nelmes, Jill (ed.),
Introduction to Film Studies,
Routledge, 1996
Deals with several national cinemas
and key concepts in film study

Nowell-Smith, Geoffrey (ed.),
The Oxford History of World Cinema,
Oxford University Press, 1996
Hugely detailed and wide-ranging
with many features on 'stars'

Thomson, David, *A Biographical Dictionary of the Cinema*, Secker & Warburg, 1975
Unashamedly driven by personal taste, but often stimulating

Truffaut, François, *Hitchcock*, Simon & Schuster, 1966, rev. edn, Touchstone, 1985
Landmark extended interview

Turner, Graeme, *Film as Social Practice*, 2nd edn, Routledge, 1993
Chapter four, 'Film Narrative', discusses structuralist theories of narrative

Wollen, Peter, *Signs and Meaning in the Cinema*, Viking, 1972
An important study in semiology

Readers should also explore the many relevant websites and journals. *Film Education* and *Sight and Sound* are standard reading.

Valuable websites include:

The Internet Movie Database at
http://uk.imdb.com

Screensite at
http://www.tcf.ua.edu/screensite/contents.html

The Media and Communications Site at the University of Aberystwyth at
http://www.aber.ac.uk/~dgc/welcome.html

There are obviously many other university and studio websites which are worth exploring in relation to film studies.

fear eats the soul

Braad Thomsen, Christien, *Fassbinder: The Life and Work of a Provocative Genius*, Faber and Faber, 1997
Provides an intelligent and personal insight into both the life and work of Fassbinder

Combs, Richard, *Monthly Film Bulletin*, Nov 1974, pp. 243–4

Cook, Pam (ed.), *The Cinema Book*, BFI, 1985
Invaluable starting point for study of melodrama

Corrigan, Timothy, *New German Film: The Displaced Image*, Austin, UT Press, 1983

Crimp, Douglas, *Fassbinder, Franz, Fox, Elvira, Erwin, Armin and All the Others*, October, No. 21, Summer 1982, pp. 63–81

Elsaesser, Thomas, *Fassbinder's Germany*, 1996
Seminal author on Fassbinder

– – –, *New German Cinema: A History*, New Brunswick, Rutgers University Press, 1989

– – –, *Introduction to BFI/NFT Fassbinder Lives! Conference*, 1999

Hayman, Ronald, *Fassbinder Filmmaker*, Simon and Schuster, 1984

Katz, Robert, *Love is Colder Than Death: The Life and Times of Rainer Werner Fassbinder*, Jonathan Cape, 1987

Lorenz, Juliane, *Chaos as Usual: Conversations about Rainer Werner Fassbinder*, Applause, 1997

Macbean, James Roy,
'The Success and Failure of RWF',
Sight and Sound, Vol. 52, No.1,
Winter 82/83

Medhurst, Andy, 'The Long Take',
Sight and Sound, Vol. 6, No. 2,
February 1996, pp. 20–22

Rayns, T. (ed.), *Fassbinder,*
British Film Institute, London, 1976

Reimer, Robert C.,
Literature Film Quarterly,
Vol. 24, No. 3, 1996
    Analysis of Fassbinder's reading of
    All That Heaven Allows

Sobchack, Thomas and Vivien C.,
An Introduction to Film,
Little, Brown and Co., 1980

Toteberg, Michael, and Lensing, Leo
(eds), *The Anarchy of the Imagination:
Interviews, Essays, Notes,*
Jon Hopkins University Press, 1992

Vincendeau, Ginette, (ed.),
Cassell Encyclopedia of European Film,
BFI, 1995

Watson, Wallace, *Film as Private and
Public Art,*
University of South Carolina Press, 1996

– – –, 'RWF',
Sight and Sound, June 1992, pp. 24–9

Spare Rib, No. 30, 1974
    Laura Mulvey reviews the film in her
    article 'Fear Eats the Soul'

*The International Directory of Films and
Filmmakers,* Volume 1 and Volume 2,
New York, St James Press, 1997

Internet References

Chandler, Daniel,
'An Introduction to Genre Theory'
(1997), (www document) URL
http://www.aber.ac.uk/~dgc/intgenre.html
    Brilliant and readable overview of
    genre theory

cinematic terms

auteurisme the 'authorship theory' of cinema, giving priority to the role of the director, whose personal style and vision is deemed to be the key factor. A director not accorded the status of auteur may be known as a metteur-en-scène

Classic Hollywood the mainstream American film industry and its products as it existed from approximately 1930–1960

closure the impression of completeness and finality achieved at the end of a literary or filmic work

continuity editing (also classical continuity) the editing technique most favoured by Hollywood and generally throughout the world, continuity editing seeks to create the illusion of seamless action, movement, and, ultimately, narrative. It does so by deploying a strategy consisting of procedures which, in direct contradiction to montage theory, hides (or at least minimises) the shift from one cut to the next, in effect making the edit as 'transparent' as possible

counterculture overlapping with the New Left, though not always political, the counterculture was a movement of revolt among mainly middle-class youth. Long hair was one of its symbolic badges; rock music and drugs signalled its iconoclastic energy

diegesis a term used in film criticism and theory, it designates the totality of the physical world experienced by the characters in a film. For example, if a character slams a door on screen and the sound of the door is heard on the sound track, the sound would be called a diegetic because we would have seen the justification for the sound on the screen, as would a character in the film. On the other hand, a sudden upsurge of violins under a tender love-scene would be called a non-diegetic sound, unless the lovebirds were seen sitting by the fiddlers who were making the music. Diegesis is not, however, limited to sounds. The credits of a film, for instance, obviously not perceived by the characters but clearly so by the spectator, would be another example of non-diegetic material

eclectic 'multiply sourced' – an eclectic work will draw on a variety of styles and ideas

fade the screen image is faded-out, usually to black, before the next image is faded in. It implies a longer time lapse than a dissolve

iconography the expressive pictorial motifs often associated with a genre. *Easy Rider* draws on the iconography of the Western

long shot this includes at least the full figures of the subjects and retains both spatial and emotional distance from the characters

long take not to be confused with 'long shot', a long take is measured in temporal rather than spatial terms. What this means is, simply, that long takes comprise shot where the camera is left running for a long period of time. As in all other aspects of life, time in film is relative: a shot which lasts 90 seconds may well be designated as a long take, though some film-makers (Renoir, Welles, Altman and others), have filmed takes of considerably greater length

metonymy an object in the normal mise-en-scène which stands for some

cinematic terms

important plot event, emotion, or theme. For example, a baby, a gun, a threatening sound

mise-en-scène taken from the theatrical practice of scene setting, this term in film analysis refers to whatever is included in the frame – it does not refer to the way in which components such as setting, lighting, props and costumes are shot

off screen space space beyond frame lines, beyond horizon, behind camera. This space is always being manipulated dramatically

shot reverse shot used to establish eye line contact and point of view in dialogue, the camera is positioned at first from the point of view of one character and then from the point of view of the other

credits

director
Rainer Werner Fassbinder

producer
Rainer Werner Fassbinder

screenplay
Rainer Werner Fassbinder

cinematography
Jürgen Jürges

film editing
Thea Eymèsz

production design
Rainer Werner Fassbinder

make-up department
Helga Kempke

production management
Christian Hohoff

second unit director or assistant director
Rainer Langhans

sound department
Fritz Müller-Scherz

lighting
Thomas Schwan

cast
Emmi Kurowski – Brigitte Mira

Ali – El Hedi ben Salem

Krista – Irm Hermann

Eugen – Rainer Werner Fassbinder

Mrs Kargus – Elma Karlowa

Mrs Ellis – Anita Bucher

Paula – Gusti Kreissl

Mrs Angermeyer – Doris Mathes

Hedwig – Margit Symo

Girl in bar – Katharina Herberg

Marquard Bohm Gruber – Peter Gauhe Bruno

Waiter – Hannes Gromball

Rudolf Waldemar Brem – Hark Bohm

Barbara – Barbara Valentin

Lilo Pempeit

Walter Sedlmayr

Karl Scheydt

Peter Moland